This page is dedicated to **P'TACH's** entire staff of professionals who have truly changed the lives of our learning disabled children. Their untiring efforts have helped create an evergrowing awareness of the plight of these precious youngsters. May Hashem grant them and all those who are supporters of **P'TACH** the strength to continue their superb work.

The Executive Board, Parents and Children of P'TACH

P'TACH
Parents for Torah for All Children

4612 Thirteenth Avenue
Brooklyn, New York 11219
(718) 854-8600

— BRINGING OUR LEARNING-DISABLED CHILDREN INTO THE MAINSTREAM OF JEWISH LIFE —

In honor of

Chana Swenson

A girl with beauty and courage

Continue being the way you are

The Sopher Family

Marilyn, Morris, Barbara, Jonathan and Lisa

In loving memory of

אסתר מלכה בת ר' יואל ע"ה

Esther Shulman

דוב בער בן ר' יצחק אייזיק שולמאן ע"ה

Bernard Shulman

חיים יהושע בן דוב בער שולמאן ע"ה

Herbert J. Shulman

יחזקאל בן ר' שלום אהרון הכהן ע"ה

Charles Kaplan

אלתר ברכה בת יצחק יוסף ע"ה

Bertha Kaplan

Arthur and Marilyn Shulman and Family

Bayonne, New Jersey

In loving memory of

a dear wife, mother, and grandmother

שרה רחל בת ר' מנשה ע"ה

Sarah Rae Brovender

Isidore Brovender

Mordechai and Shoshana Summer and Family

Chaim and Miriam Brovender and Family

ArtScroll Youth Series ®

Expositions on Jewish liturgy and thought

Rabbi Nosson Scherman
Rabbi Meir Zlotowitz
General Editors

Published by

Mesorah Publications, ltd.

ARTSCROLL YOUTH PIRKEI AVOS

New simplified translation and commentary by
Rabbi Avie Gold

Drawings by
Andras Halasz

Airbrush illustration by
Michael Horen

Designed by
Rabbi Sheah Brander

This Pirkei Avos is dedicated
to the memory of

Rabbi Meir Levi ז"ל
כ"ד חשון תשכ"ט

Rebbetzin Shoshana Levi ע"ה
י"ג כסלו תשל"ט

Pioneers and molders of girls' chinuch in America,
they founded, led, taught — and set sterling personal examples —
in the Bais Yaakov of Brownsville, East New York, and Crown Heights.

By creating Camp Hedvah, they showed
how much an intelligently crafted summer can enrich a girl's life.

Their tradition lives on in Bais Yaakov d'Rav Meir and Camp Hedvah
where their legacy of והעמידו תלמידים הרבה *continues to thrive in their children.*

תנצב"ה

FIRST EDITION
First Impression . . . March, 1989

Published and Distributed by
MESORAH PUBLICATIONS, Ltd. / Brooklyn, N.Y. 11232

Distributed in Israel by MESORAH MAFITZIM / J. GROSSMAN
Rechov Harav Uziel 117 / Jerusalem, Israel

Distributed in Europe by J. LEHMANN HEBREW BOOKSELLERS
20 Cambridge Terrace / Gateshead, Tyne and Wear / England NE8 1RP

ARTSCROLL MESORAH SERIES®
YOUTH PIRKEI AVOS (vol. 1)
© Copyright 1989, by MESORAH PUBLICATIONS, Ltd. / 4401 Second Avenue / Brooklyn, N.Y. 11232 / (718) 921-9000

ISBN: 0-89906-244-X (hard cover)
ISBN: 0-89906-245-8 (paperback)

Typography by CompuScribe at ArtScroll Studios, Ltd.
4401 Second Avenue / Brooklyn, N.Y. 11232 / (718) 921-9000

Printed in the United States of America by Edison Lithographing & Printing

❧ Avos — the Doorway to Torah and Life

by Rabbi Nosson Scherman

When the cold winter days are gone and the sun is setting later, it is time to get ready learn *Pirkei Avos* every *Shabbos* afternoon. From *Pesach* until *Rosh Hashanah,* in our homes, synagogues, and study halls, we open our hearts to *Pirkei Avos*. This slim volume of the *Mishnah* is filled with rules of wise conduct and proper behavior, with short and sharp lessons that guide us in everyday life.

How is *Pirkei Avos* different from other collections of ethical sayings by wise men?

Someone once asked Rabbi Yitchok Ze'ev Soloveitchick, the famous Brisker *Rav,* "Our Sages always speak about the importance of good character and proper behavior towards our fellow human beings. They teach that losing one's temper is like worshiping idols; that shaming another person is like killing him; and that God does not like people who brag or think they are better than others. The list of such teachings is endless. But if they are truly so important, why are the requirements of good character and conduct not listed among the 613 *mitzvos* of the Torah?"

The Brisker *Rav* answered, "The Torah was given to people, not animals. A person cannot fulfill the *mitzvos* of the Torah unless he conquers and controls the animal in himself."

This idea is as old as the Torah itself. If someone truly wishes to serve God, he must rid himself of selfishness and self-interest.

Let us imagine that two different people are studying the following passage of the Talmud: "One who wishes to be pious and of extra fine character should fulfill the teachings of *Nezikin,* the section of the Talmud that deals with laws of damages and property" (*Bava Kamma* 30a).

Even a bad person would want to study these laws very carefully. Such a person cares only about himself, and he will want to know the law so that he will know how to protect himself. Such people want to know how *not* to pay for what they do wrong, how to write contracts in words that will make them a lot of profit, even if they make someone else lose money. On the other hand, a good person will study *Nezikin,* too — but for the opposite reason. He wants to improve himself. He wants to learn how to avoid causing injury to other people and their property. He will not keep a penny to which another human being has a just claim. Obviously, when the Talmud says that good character depends on studying these laws, it is speaking to "people, not animals." A bad person can use his learning to hurt other people. A good person will study the difficult laws of *Nezikin* to discover God's rules of fair dealing and property rights, not to find ways to twist the Torah into a web that traps innocent victims.

The same passage of the Talmud continues, "One who wishes to be pious and of extra fine character should study *Avos.*" By building his character on the teachings of *Avos,* one lifts himself out of the jungle where personal survival and success are the only things that count.

A person who has studied the lessons of *Avos* will have different goals than a person who is selfish, who says "I come first," and who cares only about getting what he wants. Clearly, there is a spiritual greatness in people who live according to such lessons of *Avos* as Hillel's: "Do not judge another person until you are in his place" (2:5); or Rabban Yochanan ben Zakkai's: "Even if you have studied much Torah, do not be boastful, for that is what you were created to do" (2:9).

Let no one think, however, that the lessons of *Avos* are merely the wise teachings of good people. Many good people write books about self-improvement — and they usually disagree with each other. But, *Pirkei Avos* is not just a book, it is a part of the Torah!

In Jewish tradition, a great teacher must combine high degrees of Torah knowledge, piety, and devotion to his fellow men. Their attitudes and thoughts come from their study of Torah and their service of God. That is why the ideas and teachings of such people are true even when they discuss topics that are not related to their studies or when they offer no proof for their ideas.

The teachings of *Avos* are the accumulated wisdom of such people. They are the ones that God had in mind when He said, "Let us make man in Our image after Our likeness" (*Bereishis* 1:26). This is why, for the nation of Torah, the sayings of a Hillel, and Rabban Yochanan ben Zakkai and the other Sages in *Avos* are as true as God's Own word.

Only the experts in any field can set forth the rules for success in their field. We do not ask accountants to train artists or plumbers to teach cooking. So, too, only the great Torah figures could draw the road map to be followed when searching for human perfection. That is why *Avos* is so different from collections of ethical sayings by the wise men of other nations, and from other books on self-improvement. All of the teachings in *Avos* have their roots in the Torah itself.

And that is why *Avos* begins with the words, "Moshe received the Torah from [Hashem at] Mount Sinai."

פִּרְקֵי אָבוֹת — *Pirkei Avos*

Pirkei Avos teaches us how we should act toward other people and toward *Hashem*. These lessons may be called "good conduct" or "proper behavior." Sometimes they are called "ethics."

But who knows which conduct is good and which is bad? Who can tell us which behavior is proper and which is not? The answer is: *Hashem* knows; *Hashem* can teach us. And He did teach us when He gave us the Torah.

The Torah teaches us many *mitzvos* about how to treat other people and how to serve *Hashem*. And the Torah also tells us many stories about such great men as Avraham, Yitzchak and Yaakov who are called the אָבוֹת, *Fathers*, of the Jewish people, and such great women as Sarah, Rivkah, Rachel and Leah who are called our אִמָהוֹת, *Mothers*. These stories tell us how these *tzaddikim* behaved toward others. For example, we read about Avraham and Sarah and the wonderful חֶסֶד, *kindness*, they showed to everyone they met, even strangers.

Many of the lessons that we learn about Jewish "ethics" can be found in these stories. That is why we call these lessons *Pirkei Avos*, which means the "Chapters of the Fathers." In other words, *Pirkei Avos* teaches the lessons of proper behavior that we learn from the stories of our *Avos*.

Many people study or recite *Pirkei Avos* every *Shabbos* afternoon during the summer. They study one chapter each week between *Pesach* and *Rosh Hashanah*. In this way *Pirkei Avos* is reviewed four times each year. The weekly chapter is introduced with the following *mishnah* which is taken from *Sanhedrin* 10:1.

All Jews have a share in the World to Come. In the words of the *Navi (Yishayahu* 60:21), "Your people are all righteous *tzaddikim;* they shall inherit the land forever. They are the branch of My planting, they are the work of My hands, in which to take pride."

כָּל יִשְׂרָאֵל יֵשׁ לָהֶם חֵלֶק לְעוֹלָם הַבָּא, שֶׁנֶּאֱמַר: "וְעַמֵּךְ כֻּלָּם צַדִּיקִים, לְעוֹלָם יִירְשׁוּ אָרֶץ, נֵצֶר מַטָּעַי, מַעֲשֵׂה יָדַי לְהִתְפָּאֵר."

The weekly chapter is followed by the following *mishnah* which is taken from *Makkos* 3:18.

R' Chanania ben Akashia taught: *Hashem,* the Holy One, Blessed is He, wished to reward the Jewish people. That is why he gave them such a large Torah and so many *mitzvos.* This is what the *Navi (Yishayahu* 42:21) taught, "*Hashem* desired that the Jews should be righteous *tzaddikim,* therefore he enlarged and strengthened the Torah.

רַבִּי חֲנַנְיָא בֶּן עֲקַשְׁיָא אוֹמֵר: רָצָה הַקָּדוֹשׁ בָּרוּךְ הוּא לְזַכּוֹת אֶת יִשְׂרָאֵל, לְפִיכָךְ הִרְבָּה לָהֶם תּוֹרָה וּמִצְוֹת, שֶׁנֶּאֱמַר: "ה' חָפֵץ לְמַעַן צִדְקוֹ, יַגְדִּיל תּוֹרָה וְיַאְדִּיר."

1. Moshe received the Torah from Hashem at Mount Sinai. Moshe taught the Torah to Yehoshua and trained him to be the next leader of the Jews. Yehoshua taught it to the Elders who became the leaders after him. The Elders taught the Torah to the Prophets. The Prophets taught the Torah to the group of Sages known as the *Anshei Knesses Hagedolah.*

The *Anshei Knesses Hagedolah* taught three important lessons: (a) Think very carefully before judging. (b) Teach as many students as possible. (c) Make a fence to protect the Torah.

[א] **מֹשֶׁה** קִבֵּל תּוֹרָה מִסִּינַי. וּמְסָרָהּ לִיהוֹשֻׁעַ. וִיהוֹשֻׁעַ לִזְקֵנִים. וּזְקֵנִים לִנְבִיאִים. וּנְבִיאִים מְסָרוּהָ לְאַנְשֵׁי כְנֶסֶת הַגְּדוֹלָה.

הֵם אָמְרוּ שְׁלֹשָׁה דְבָרִים: הֱווּ מְתוּנִים בַּדִּין. וְהַעֲמִידוּ תַלְמִידִים הַרְבֵּה. וַעֲשׂוּ סְיָג לַתּוֹרָה.

---

1. מֹשֶׁה קִבֵּל תּוֹרָה מִסִּינַי — Moshe received the Torah from Hashem at Mount Sinai.

Some people are arrogant, others are humble. Arrogant people think they are the smartest in the world. They expect everybody to do things their way. They boast and brag about how great they are. And, of course, they never apologize for their mistakes. *Hashem* does not like arrogant people.

The opposite of arrogant is humble. People who are humble never boast or brag. They are very careful not to hurt others or make them feel bad. They seek advice and are thankful for it. *Hashem* loves humble people. Moshe was the most humble man who ever lived. That is why *Hashem* chose Moshe to receive the Torah for the Jews.

The *Gemara* (*Megillah* 29a; *Sotah* 5a) learns this lesson from the mountains around *Eretz Yisrael*. *Hashem* chose to give the Torah on Mount Sinai. Then two very tall mountains, Tavor and Carmel, came to complain. "We are taller and more beautiful than Mount Sinai," they said arrogantly. "*Hashem* should give the Torah on us!"

But *Hashem* does not like arrogance. That is why he chose Mount Sinai, a "humble" mountain.

Moshe understood this lesson and he became even more humble. That is why *Pirkei Avos* begins: מֹשֶׁה קִבֵּל תּוֹרָה מִסִּינַי, *Moshe received the Torah from Sinai.* He learned from Mount Sinai that only a humble person is worthy of receiving the Torah.

וּמְסָרָהּ לִיהוֹשֻׁעַ — Moshe taught the Torah to Yehoshua.

To learn proper behavior we must have expert teachers. The lessons of *Pirkei Avos* were taught by experts. Even more, these teachers followed their own lessons. They were wonderful examples of how good people behave. These teachers were called *Tannaim* and each one was called a *Tanna*. Each of their lessons is called a *mishnah*.

The *Tannaim* learned how to behave from their teachers. And their teachers had learned from their teachers, all the way back to the greatest teacher, Moshe *Rabbeinu*, who learned from *Hashem* Himself.

When Moshe grew old, he asked *Hashem* who the next leader of the Jews would be. *Hashem* said that it would be Yehoshua.

Yehoshua was perfect for this job. He was Moshe's best student. He went wherever Moshe went. He listened to every word Moshe spoke. He watched everything Moshe did. And so he became a great leader like Moshe. We learn about his leadership in *Sefer Yehoshua*, the Book of Joshua.

וִיהוֹשֻׁעַ לִזְקֵנִים — Yehoshua taught it to the Elders.

After Yehoshua died, a group of wise men became the leaders of the nation. They were called "Zekeinim" or "Elders". They ruled for almost three hundred years. We do not know most of their names, but we do know some. We have all heard stories about Pinchas the grandson of Aharon, Boaz who married Rus, Elkanah father of Shmuel, Shimshon with his great strength, and the prophetess Devorah. We read about them in *Sefer Shoftim*, the Book of Judges.

לִנְבִיאִים — To the Prophets.

The period of the *Neviim*, or Prophets, began with Eli the *Kohein* and his student Shmuel. It ended about six hundred years later, soon after the Second *Beis Hamikdash* was built. Among the *Neviim* were Eliyahu, Elisha, Yishayahu, Yirmiyahu, Yechezkel, Yonah, Mordechai and Esther. Most of Tanach tells us about the *Neviim* and their teachings.

לְאַנְשֵׁי כְנֶסֶת הַגְּדוֹלָה — To the group of Sages known as the *Anshei Knesses Hagedolah*.

In the early years of the Second *Beis Hamikdash*, the leader of the Jews in *Eretz Yisrael* was Ezra *Hakohein*. He was also called Ezra *Hasofer*, the Scribe, because he wrote Torah scrolls.

Ezra had a *beis din*, or court, to help him rule. The members of Ezra's *beis din* were known as the *Anshei Knesses Hagedolah* or "the Men of the Great Assembly." This group had one hundred and twenty members, some of whom were *Neviim*. Among the more famous ones were: Daniel and his companions — Chananiah, Mishael and Azariah; Mordechai of the Purim story; Chaggai, Zechariah and Malachi, the last of the prophets; and Shimon *Hatzaddik* whom we will meet in the next *mishnah*.

הֵם אָמְרוּ שְׁלֹשָׁה דְבָרִים — They taught three important lessons.

Certainly, the *Anshei Knesses Hagedolah* taught more than just three lessons. But these three are important for the future of Torah:

If a judge in *beis din* does not "think very carefully before

Moshe received the Torah . . . at Mount Sinai.

judging,'' then he may not judge correctly. People will think that the Torah is to blame for his wrong judgment.

If the community does not set up many Torah schools to ''teach as many students as possible,'' then many people will grow up without knowing any Torah.

If the Torah leaders don't ''make a fence to protect the Torah,'' then ignorant people will sin without realizing what they are doing.

That is why these three lessons are so very important.

וַעֲשׂוּ סְיָג לַתּוֹרָה — And make a fence to protect the Torah.

Some *mitzvos* tell us what we must do. Others tell us what we must not do. Sometimes we may make a mistake and do the wrong thing or forget to do the right thing.

The wise Torah Sages made many rules that help us remember the *mitzvos* and stop us from making mistakes. For example, the Torah tells us not to write on *Shabbos*. So the Sages made the rule that we must not even pick up a pencil on *Shabbos*. If we do hold pencils in our hands, we might forget and write.

This kind of rule is called a סְיָג, *fence*. Just as a fence stops us from entering a place where we should not be, so do these rules stop us from doing what we should not do.

But every person is different. And so every person may make a different kind of mistake. Therefore, every person should make his own ''fences'' that will help him to do the *mitzvos* properly.

2. After most of the older members of the *Anshei Knesses Hagedolah* grew old and passed away, Shimon *Hatzaddik* was one of the last remaining members. He taught:

The world was created so that we should do three things and without these three things the world could not exist: (a) We should study Torah. (b) We should serve *Hashem*. (c) We should act kindly to others.

[ב] שִׁמְעוֹן הַצַּדִּיק הָיָה מִשְּׁיָרֵי כְנֶסֶת הַגְּדוֹלָה. הוּא הָיָה אוֹמֵר: עַל שְׁלשָׁה דְבָרִים הָעוֹלָם עוֹמֵד: עַל הַתּוֹרָה. וְעַל הָעֲבוֹדָה. וְעַל גְּמִילוּת חֲסָדִים.

Serve Hashem.

Study Torah.

Act kindly.

2. שִׁמְעוֹן הַצַּדִּיק — **Shimon Hatzaddik.**

Shimon *Hatzaddik* was among the last and youngest of the Sages to join the *Anshei Knesses Hagedolah*. For this reason he outlived most of the others. He was the *Kohein Gadol* for forty years. During that time many miracles happened in the *Beis Hamikdash*. But when Shimon *Hatzaddik* died, the miracles stopped.

עַל שְׁלֹשָׁה דְבָרִים הָעוֹלָם עוֹמֵד — **The world was created so that we should do three things.**

Each of us must act properly towards himself, towards *Hashem*, and towards other people. We must improve ourselves by learning Torah. We must serve *Hashem* through prayer and doing *mitzvos*. We must treat other people with kindness and respect.

3. Antigonus of Socho learned Torah from Shimon *Hatzaddik.* Antigonus taught:

You should not act like servants who only serve their master because they want to receive a reward. Rather, you should act like servants who serve their master because they love him and serve him without even thinking about a reward. Yet, although you love *Hashem* and wish to be close to Him, you should still fear Him so that you will not sin.

4. Yose ben Yo'ezer of Tzereidah and Yose ben Yochanan of Yerushalayim learned Torah from Shimon *Hatzaddik* and Antigonus of Socho.

Yose ben Yo'ezer of Tzereidah taught: Let your home be a meeting place for wise men; become dusty with the dust of their feet; and drink their words like a thirsty man drinks water.

5. Yose ben Yochanan of Yerushalayim taught: (a) The door of your home should be opened wide so that guests may enter easily. (b) You should treat poor people as if they were members of your family. (c) You should not chatter too much with a woman.

[ג] אַנְטִיגְנוֹס אִישׁ סוֹכוֹ קִבֵּל מִשִּׁמְעוֹן הַצַּדִיק. הוּא הָיָה אוֹמֵר:
אַל תִּהְיוּ כַּעֲבָדִים הַמְשַׁמְּשִׁין אֶת הָרַב עַל מְנָת לְקַבֵּל פְּרָס. אֶלָּא, הֱווּ כַּעֲבָדִים הַמְשַׁמְּשִׁין אֶת הָרַב שֶׁלֹּא עַל מְנָת לְקַבֵּל פְּרָס. וִיהִי מוֹרָא שָׁמַיִם עֲלֵיכֶם.

[ד] יוֹסֵי בֶּן יוֹעֶזֶר אִישׁ צְרֵדָה וְיוֹסֵי בֶּן יוֹחָנָן אִישׁ יְרוּשָׁלַיִם קִבְּלוּ מֵהֶם.
יוֹסֵי בֶּן יוֹעֶזֶר אִישׁ צְרֵדָה אוֹמֵר: יְהִי בֵיתְךָ בֵּית וַעַד לַחֲכָמִים, וֶהֱוֵי מִתְאַבֵּק בַּעֲפַר רַגְלֵיהֶם, וֶהֱוֵי שׁוֹתֶה בַצָּמָא אֶת דִּבְרֵיהֶם.

[ה] יוֹסֵי בֶּן יוֹחָנָן אִישׁ יְרוּשָׁלַיִם אוֹמֵר: יְהִי בֵיתְךָ פָּתוּחַ לִרְוָחָה. וְיִהְיוּ עֲנִיִּים בְּנֵי בֵיתֶךָ. וְאַל תַּרְבֶּה שִׂיחָה עִם הָאִשָּׁה.

---

3. אַל תִּהְיוּ כַּעֲבָדִים — **You should not act like servants . . .**

Why do we obey instructions or follow orders from another person? There are times when we obey because of love. We love that person who gives the orders and we know that that person loves us. We love our mother and father and we show this love by obeying them.

Sometimes we follow orders because of fear. We are afraid that something bad will happen if we disobey. When the school crossing guard tells us to wait, we wait. We fear that if we didn't listen, terrible things could happen. We've all seen children wearing casts or walking with crutches after being hit by a car. May *Hashem* protect us from such things.

Often we do not really care to follow another person's orders. We have no special love for that person and we are not afraid of him. Yet we listen, because when we do we receive a reward. A worker does not have to love or fear his boss. But if he wants to get paid, he must do what the boss tells him.

We should not obey *Hashem* because we wish to receive a reward. That is not the best reason to serve *Hashem*. We should serve Him because we love Him, and we show that love by doing His *mitzvos*.

4. וֶהֱוֵי מִתְאַבֵּק בַּעֲפַר רַגְלֵיהֶם — **Become dusty with the dust of their feet.**

When a person walks on an unpaved road, his feet kick up the dust. If another person follows closely behind him, the second one will become covered with dust. The *Tanna* teaches that you should follow the lessons of the wise men very carefully and very closely. Then it will be as if you are walking in the dust they kicked up, and you will become full of their wisdom.

There is another explanation of this *mishnah*. In olden times the teacher would sit on a chair or a bench and the students would sit around him on the ground. Here we are taught to sit at the feet of the wise teachers so that we may learn from them.

5. וְיִהְיוּ עֲנִיִּים בְּנֵי בֵיתֶךָ — **You should treat poor people as if they were members of your family.**

Nobody enjoys being poor and receiving charity. When we help other people, we should be careful not to make them feel bad.

Here's an example: A boy has outgrown his *Shabbos* suit, but it is still in pretty good condition. His mother tells him to bring it to a poor family around the corner. He should not hand them the suit and say, "Here's an old suit that I don't need anymore!" That would make them feel very sad. Instead, he should say, "This suit no longer fits me, but I think it would look very good on you and you will enjoy wearing it."

וְאַל תַּרְבֶּה שִׂיחָה עִם הָאִשָּׁה — **You should not chatter too much with a woman.**

A husband and wife should enjoy speaking with one another. They should take pleasure in planning together to make their home "opened wide so that guests may enter easily." They should happily discuss how to "treat poor people as if they were members of the family." They should find delight in hearing each other's opinions about how to teach their children good *middos*.

Sometimes they should even make light conversation about not-so-serious matters. But this should not take up too much of their time, because a man who truly respects his wife will offer her much more than just idle chatter.

This last rule was taught even about a man's own wife, certainly it is true about another man's wife. From this the Sages learned another lesson: A man who chatters too much with women could cause bad things to happen to himself. He could leave his Torah studies, and he could end up in *Gehinnom*.

6. Yehoshua ben Perachyah and Nittai of Arbel learned Torah from Yose ben Yo'ezer and Yose ben Yochanan.

Yehoshua ben Perachyah taught: (a) Appoint a Torah teacher for yourself. (b) Gain a friend for yourself. (c) Judge all people in a good way.

7. Nittai of Arbel taught: (a) Stay far away from a bad neighbor. (b) Do not be friends with a bad person. (c) Do not think that a bad person will escape his punishment.

בְּאִשְׁתּוֹ אָמְרוּ, קַל וָחֹמֶר בְּאֵשֶׁת חֲבֵרוֹ. מִכַּאן אָמְרוּ חֲכָמִים: כָּל הַמַּרְבֶּה שִׂיחָה עִם הָאִשָּׁה — גּוֹרֵם רָעָה לְעַצְמוֹ. וּבוֹטֵל מִדִּבְרֵי תוֹרָה, וְסוֹפוֹ יוֹרֵשׁ גֵּיהִנֹּם.

[ו] יְהוֹשֻׁעַ בֶּן פְּרַחְיָה וְנִתַּאי הָאַרְבֵּלִי קִבְּלוּ מֵהֶם.

יְהוֹשֻׁעַ בֶּן פְּרַחְיָה אוֹמֵר: עֲשֵׂה לְךָ רַב. וּקְנֵה לְךָ חָבֵר. וֶהֱוֵי דָן אֶת כָּל הָאָדָם לְכַף זְכוּת.

[ז] נִתַּאי הָאַרְבֵּלִי אוֹמֵר: הַרְחֵק מִשָּׁכֵן רָע. וְאַל תִּתְחַבֵּר לָרָשָׁע. וְאַל תִּתְיָאֵשׁ מִן הַפֻּרְעָנוּת.

6. עֲשֵׂה לְךָ רַב — Appoint a Torah teacher for yourself.

It is very difficult for a person to learn Torah by himself. He can never be sure if he correctly understands what he is studying, or if his mind is playing tricks on him. But, if he learns from a teacher (who has also learned from his teacher), then he becomes part of the great chain of Torah students that stretches all the way back to Moshe *Rabbeinu*.

וּקְנֵה לְךָ חָבֵר — Gain a friend for yourself.

The word קְנֵה means "gain" but can also mean "buy". This means that a person should do whatever is necessary to win over a friend. There are many reasons why people need good friends. Here's one example.

A person may have a bad habit. He may not even realize that he has it. Most people would not bother to correct him. They would tell themselves,"It's not my business!" Or, "I don't care about that guy anyway!" But a good friend will not say these things. He will speak to his friend about this bad habit and will help him to change his ways. If a person does not have such friends, he should hire someone to be the kind of friend that will correct him when he does the wrong thing.

Another meaning of this *mishnah* is: When you study Torah, it is always better to do so with a חַבְרוּתָא, *chavrusa* or partner, than to study by yourself. That way if one of you makes a mistake, his partner will correct him. This is what Shlomo *Hamelech* meant when he wrote [*Mishlei* 4:9], "טוֹבִים הַשְּׁנַיִם מִן הָאֶחָד, Two are better than one." Our *mishnah* teaches that if you cannot find a partner to learn with, you should pay someone to be your study-partner.

וֶהֱוֵי דָן אֶת כָּל הָאָדָם לְכַף זְכוּת — Judge all people in a good way.

Here is an example. One day, Yehudis and Rivkah were waiting for the school bus. "I wonder what happened to Elisheva today!" Said Yehudis. "She's always the first one at the bus stop." When they were on the bus, Yehudis suddenly pointed out the window. "Look Rivkah, there's Elisheva! I wonder where she's going!"

Rivkah was very quick with her answer, "She must be playing hookey today. I'll bet her mother sent her to the bus on time and she walked very slowly. She missed the bus on purpose!"

"What are you saying, Rivkah?" said Yehudis. "You are speaking *lashon hara*, bad things, about Elisheva! Maybe her mother asked her to run an errand! Maybe something important happened! We must always judge people in a good way!"

You can imagine how surprised the two girls were when Elisheva came into class half an hour late. "Why are you so late this morning, Elisheva?" the teacher asked.

Elisheva answered, "Mrs. Goldstein called our house this morning. She is sick and had no milk for her children's breakfast. So Mother sent me to her house with a container of milk. That's why I missed the school bus today."

The teacher noticed Rivkah's face turn red, but she was wise enough and kind enough not to ask her about it.

7. הַרְחֵק מִשָּׁכֵן רָע וְאַל תִּתְחַבֵּר לָרָשָׁע — Stay far away from a bad neighbor; (and) do not be friends with a bad person.

If someone enters a room in which many people are smoking cigarettes, his clothing will soon smell from smoke. When he walks out of the room other people will think that he had been smoking also. But he did not smoke. The same thing happens with a person who stays in the company of bad neighbors and bad friends. Soon his *neshamah* and his reputation will become dirtied by their sins. When they are punished he may be punished along with them. Therefore we must stay far away from such people.

. . . if they have accepted the ruling.

8. Yehudah ben Tabbai and Shimon ben Shatach learned Torah from Yehoshua ben Perachayah and Nittai of Arbel.

Yehudah ben Tabbai taught these lessons for judges: (a) Do not act as a lawyer. (b) When the two sides stand before you, think of them both as guilty. (c) Once the two of them have left your courtroom, think of them both as innocent — if they have accepted the ruling.

[ח] יְהוּדָה בֶּן טַבַּאי וְשִׁמְעוֹן בֶּן שָׁטַח קִבְּלוּ מֵהֶם.

יְהוּדָה בֶּן טַבַּאי אוֹמֵר: אַל תַּעַשׂ עַצְמְךָ כְּעוֹרְכֵי הַדַּיָּנִין. וּכְשֶׁיִּהְיוּ בַּעֲלֵי הַדִּין עוֹמְדִים לְפָנֶיךָ, יִהְיוּ בְעֵינֶיךָ כִּרְשָׁעִים. וּכְשֶׁנִּפְטָרִים מִלְּפָנֶיךָ, יִהְיוּ בְעֵינֶיךָ כְּזַכָּאִין, כְּשֶׁקִּבְּלוּ עֲלֵיהֶם אֶת הַדִּין.

8. אַל תַּעַשׂ עַצְמְךָ כְּעוֹרְכֵי הַדַּיָּנִין — **Do not act as a lawyer.**
A lawyer helps a person prepare his case before the court. He tells his client (the person he is helping) what things to say, and what things not to say. But a judge may not do this. He must listen to what each person says, without suggesting that he say something else. A judge can decide between two people only according to their own words.

יִהְיוּ בְעֵינֶיךָ כִּרְשָׁעִים — **Think of them both as guilty.**
This does not mean that the judge should accuse each one of lying. It means that he should treat them both in the same

way. Even if one of them is well known for his honesty, the judge should not say to himself, "This man never tells a lie. He must be telling the truth now also." Instead, the judge must think carefully about what each person says. Then he can make a fair judgment.

יִהְיוּ בְעֵינֶיךָ כְּזַכָּאִין — **Think of them both as innocent.**
Do not think, "The one who lost the case is a liar. He knew he was wrong and he lied in order to win." Instead, say to yourself, "He really thought he was right. He didn't lie. He made a mistake."

9. Shimon ben Shatach also taught a lesson for judges:

Ask the witnesses a lot of questions, but be careful that your words should not teach them how to lie.

10. Shemayah and Avtalyon learned Torah from Yehudah ben Tabbai and Shimon ben Shatach.

Shemayah taught: (a) You should love work. (b) You should hate being in a position of power. (c) You should not be too friendly with government officials.

11. Avtalyon taught a lesson for teachers. He said:

O wise men, be careful with your words, for someday you may be forced to leave your city to live in a place which has "bad water." When your students follow you there, they may drink that bad water and die. This will cause a *chillul Hashem.*

[ט] שִׁמְעוֹן בֶּן שָׁטַח אוֹמֵר:
הֱוֵי מַרְבֶּה לַחֲקוֹר אֶת הָעֵדִים, וֶהֱוֵי זָהִיר בִּדְבָרֶיךָ, שֶׁמָּא מִתּוֹכָם יִלְמְדוּ לְשַׁקֵּר.

[י] שְׁמַעְיָה וְאַבְטַלְיוֹן קִבְּלוּ מֵהֶם. שְׁמַעְיָה אוֹמֵר: אֱהַב אֶת הַמְּלָאכָה. וּשְׂנָא אֶת הָרַבָּנוּת. וְאַל תִּתְוַדַּע לָרָשׁוּת.

[יא] אַבְטַלְיוֹן אוֹמֵר:
חֲכָמִים, הִזָּהֲרוּ בְדִבְרֵיכֶם, שֶׁמָּא תָחוּבוּ חוֹבַת גָּלוּת וְתִגְלוּ לִמְקוֹם מַיִם הָרָעִים. וְיִשְׁתּוּ הַתַּלְמִידִים הַבָּאִים אַחֲרֵיכֶם, וְיָמוּתוּ. וְנִמְצָא שֵׁם שָׁמַיִם מִתְחַלֵּל.

9. שֶׁמָּא מִתּוֹכָם יִלְמְדוּ לְשַׁקֵּר — **Your words should not teach them how to lie.**

A mother once came into the kitchen and found that someone had cut a chunk out of her freshly baked cake. "Who took cake without permission?" she called out.

"What cake?" replied Yossi from the next room.

Later that night she asked Yossi, "How did you manage to eat that big piece of cake all by yourself?"

This time Yossi replied, "I guess I did the wrong thing, Mommy. I'm sorry."

Yossi gave a different answer when his mother asked the question differently. In the same way when the judge questions the witnesses, he must be careful of the words he uses. Otherwise his questions may teach them how to lie.

10. אֱהַב אֶת הַמְּלָאכָה — **You should love work.**

Every person must keep himself occupied. When a person has too much free time, he begins to find ways to use that time. If he fills his day with study, work and even with some healthy play, then his time is not wasted. His mind and his body always do useful things and he accomplishes a lot. But if he wastes his time sitting around doing nothing useful, his mind will soon be filled with silly ideas. Little by little, this foolishness will become the most important part of his life. According to another *mishnah* (*Kesubos* 5:5), this will lead either to sin or to insanity.

וּשְׂנָא אֶת הָרַבָּנוּת — **You should hate being in a position of power.**

Being in a position of power is not easy. First of all, a person in a powerful position may have many jealous enemies who seek to do him harm. Secondly, a powerful person must always make important decisions. A wrong decision, even if it is only a little bit wrong, can cause great problems. For example, a general must think very carefully before he leads his army into battle. If his plans go wrong, he and all of his soldiers may be captured or even killed.

Thirdly, a person in a position of power must always remember that *Hashem* put him into that position to set an example for others to follow. If he becomes selfish, or if he mistreats those under him, *Hashem* will judge him harshly. In fact, the *Gemara* (*Pesachim* 87b) tells us that kingship sometimes makes a person die young. That is why many of the prophets outlived four kings each. For example, the prophets Yeshayahu and Hoshea each prophesied during the reigns of Uziyahu, Yosam, Achaz, and Yechizkiyahu.

וְאַל תִּתְוַדַּע לָרָשׁוּת — **You should not be too friendly with government officials.**

This is explained in chapter 2, *mishnah* 3.

11. חֲכָמִים הִזָּהֲרוּ בְדִבְרֵיכֶם — **O wise men, be careful with your words.**

When you teach your students, you must choose your words carefully. Do not speak in a way that can be misunderstood. Your own students may be used to your way of teaching. They will study your lessons until they are sure that they understand exactly what you meant to say.

But someday you may have to travel to another place. In this new place you will find "bad water." That is, you will find students who will not study everything you say carefully. Instead, they will misinterpret whatever you teach. They will act sinfully and say, "We are only doing what is written in the Torah. This is what our teacher taught us." Others will learn from them, thinking that they are following the Torah.

The *mishnah* calls these false interpretations of the Torah "bad water." Just as bad water makes a person's body sick, these false teachings make a person's soul sick. And they are a *chillul Hashem*, a disgrace to God's Holy Name.

12. Hillel and Shammai learned Torah from Shemayah and Avta-lyon.

Hillel taught:

Be one of the followers of Aaron the *Kohein Gadol.* You can do this by loving peace, running after peace, loving people and bringing them closer to the Torah.

[יב] הִלֵּל וְשַׁמַּאי קִבְּלוּ מֵהֶם.
הִלֵּל אוֹמֵר: הֱוֵי מִתַּלְמִידָיו
שֶׁל אַהֲרֹן. אוֹהֵב שָׁלוֹם וְרוֹדֵף
שָׁלוֹם, אוֹהֵב אֶת הַבְּרִיּוֹת וּמְקָרְבָן
לַתּוֹרָה.

12. הֱוֵי מִתַּלְמִידָיו שֶׁל אַהֲרֹן — **Be one of the followers of Aharon the *Kohein Gadol.***

How did Aharon run after peace? Whenever Aharon saw that two people were angry at each other, he would approach one of them and say, "Do you realize how sorry your friend is for making you angry? He really is so ashamed of himself that he is too embarrassed to ask you for forgiveness. That is why he wants me to speak to you for him. Won't you please forgive him?" Then Aharon would go to the other person and say the exact same thing. And the next time the two "enemies" met they would greet each other as old friends.

How did Aharon bring people closer to the Torah? Whenever Aharon knew that a person had sinned, he would approach that person, put his hand on that person's shoulder and talk to him in a very friendly way. Usually the sinner would think, "Look how friendly Aharon is to me. He must really think I'm someone special. If he only knew about my bad ways, he would never even speak to me again. If I want Aharon to remain my friend, I'd better start behaving myself." And he would mend his ways and follow the laws more carefully.

13. Hillel also taught: (a) A person who spreads his name will lose his name. (b) A person who does not add to his Torah knowledge will forget what he already knows. (c) A person who does not study Torah at all does not deserve to live. (d) A person who uses his Torah knowledge selfishly will lose his reward.

14. Hillel also taught that we should always ask ourselves three questions: (a) If I am not for myself, who will be for me? (b) And if I am for myself, what am I? (c) And if not now, when?

15. Shammai taught: (a) Make a regular schedule for your Torah study. (b) Say a little but do a lot. (c) Greet all people cheerfully.

16. Rabban Gamliel taught: (a) Appoint a Torah teacher for yourself so that you will be free of doubt. (b) Do not guess how much *ma'aser* to give.

[יג] הוּא הָיָה אוֹמֵר: נְגִיד שְׁמָא אֲבַד שְׁמֵהּ. וּדְלָא מוֹסִיף יָסֵף. וּדְלָא יַלֵּיף קְטָלָא חַיָּב. וּדְאִשְׁתַּמֵּשׁ בְּתָגָא חֲלָף.

[יד] הוּא הָיָה אוֹמֵר: אִם אֵין אֲנִי לִי, מִי לִי? וּכְשֶׁאֲנִי לְעַצְמִי, מָה אֲנִי? וְאִם לֹא עַכְשָׁו, אֵימָתַי?

[טו] שַׁמַּאי אוֹמֵר: עֲשֵׂה תוֹרָתְךָ קֶבַע. אֱמֹר מְעַט וַעֲשֵׂה הַרְבֵּה. וֶהֱוֵי מְקַבֵּל אֶת כָּל הָאָדָם בְּסֵבֶר פָּנִים יָפוֹת.

[טז] רַבָּן גַּמְלִיאֵל הָיָה אוֹמֵר: עֲשֵׂה לְךָ רַב, וְהִסְתַּלֵּק מִן הַסָּפֵק. וְאַל תַּרְבֶּה לְעַשֵּׂר אֻמָדוֹת.

---

13. נְגִיד שְׁמָא אֲבַד שְׁמֵהּ — A person who spreads his name will lose his name.

People who always do good things often become famous and are honored by others. They may not seek fame or honor, but it comes to them anyway. A yeshivah may place their names on the school's wall. A hospital to which they have donated a large amount of money may put their name on an ambulance. They may be asked to speak or to be the guests of honor at a dinner. Their honor comes for only one reason, they are worthy of it. Such honor lasts forever.

Some people only do good deeds in order to become famous. They will not give any donations to a yeshivah, unless their name is placed on the building wall. They will not give any money to a hospital to buy a new ambulance, unless their name is printed on the side of the ambulance. They will not help with a charity dinner, unless they are allowed to make a speech at the dinner. Their charity is real charity. Their speech may even be very interesting. And their honor is real honor. But it comes for two reasons: First, because they seek it; second because they deserve it. Such honor may last very long, but at some time it will begin to fade.

וּדְלָא מוֹסִיף יָסֵף — A person who does not add to his Torah knowledge will forget what he already knows.

We must always review our Torah lessons and study new portions. In this way our Torah knowledge will grow and grow. But if someone does not do this, he will soon know less and less. In the *Gemara* (*Yerushalmi Berachos* 9:5) we are taught: "יוֹם תַּעַזְבֵנִי יוֹמַיִם אֶעֶזְבֶךָ, If you leave me (the Torah) for one day, I will leave you for two days." This is like two people who are traveling in different directions on the same road. After one day the two travelers will be two days away from each other. After two days, they will be four days apart.

וּדְאִשְׁתַּמֵּשׁ בְּתָגָא חֲלָף — A person who uses his Torah knowledge selfishly will lose his reward.

Torah study is required of everybody. At the very least, one must study the *mitzvos* that affect his everyday life. Therefore one who has gained much Torah knowledge should not use it in a selfish way. He must share his knowledge with others. Although, everyone must show respect for a Torah scholar, the scholar may not make harsh or selfish demands on others. If he does such things, then they will be considered as part of the reward for his Torah learning. And he will not get the full reward that he should have received in *Gan Eden*.

14. אִם אֵין אֲנִי לִי — If I am not for myself.

This means, if I do not fulfill the *mitzvos* that *Hashem* requires of me, will anybody else do them for me? "And even if I am for myself," and I do many *mitzvos,* how much can one person accomplish all by himself? And if I do not do as much as I can while I'm still young and full of strength and vigor, when will I be able to do it?

16. עֲשֵׂה לְךָ רַב — Appoint a Torah teacher for yourself.]

These same words appeared earlier (*mishnah* 6). There we were taught to appoint a teacher so that we would become part of the great chain of Torah students that stretches all the way back to Moshe *Rabbeinu*. Here we are taught to choose a *rav* to whom we will bring all of our questions in *halachah*. This is why the *Tanna* adds, "וְהִסְתַּלֵּק מִן הַסָּפֵק, so that you will be free of doubt." If you will choose a *rav* who will decide all of your halachic problems, then you will always be certain of the correct way to act.

וְאַל תַּרְבֶּה לְעַשֵּׂר אֻמָדוֹת — Do not guess how much ma'aser to give.

Before eating from the crops that grow in *Eretz Yisrael*, *ma'aser* must be set aside. *Ma'aser* is exactly one-tenth of the harvest and is given to a *Levi*. In order to be sure that he sets aside the proper amount for *ma'aser*, a person must first measure the size of his crop. If he is too lazy to take a correct measurement and he just guesses how much to set aside, he may not set aside enough. Or he may set aside too much. In either case, he did not fulfill the *mitzvah* of *ma'aser* properly.

Make a regular schedule for your Torah study.

17. Shimon the son of Rabban Gamliel taught: (a) All my life I have been raised among the Sages and I have not found anything better than silence. (b) Merely studying Torah is not as important as doing what the Torah tells us to do. (c) Anyone who talks too much brings on sin.

18. Rabban Shimon ben Gamliel taught:

The world continues to stand because of three things: (a) Because of truth; (b) because of justice; and (c) because of peace.

We learn this from the words of the *Navi* (*Zechariah* 8:16): "Truth and justice, peace shall rule in your gates."

[יז] שִׁמְעוֹן בְּנוֹ אוֹמֵר: כָּל יָמַי גָּדַלְתִּי בֵּין הַחֲכָמִים, וְלֹא מָצָאתִי לַגּוּף טוֹב אֶלָּא שְׁתִיקָה. וְלֹא הַמִּדְרָשׁ הוּא הָעִקָּר, אֶלָּא הַמַּעֲשֶׂה. וְכָל הַמַּרְבֶּה דְבָרִים מֵבִיא חֵטְא.

[יח] רַבָּן שִׁמְעוֹן בֶּן גַּמְלִיאֵל אוֹמֵר: עַל שְׁלֹשָׁה דְבָרִים הָעוֹלָם קַיָּם — עַל הַדִּין וְעַל הָאֱמֶת וְעַל הַשָּׁלוֹם. שֶׁנֶּאֱמַר: "אֱמֶת וּמִשְׁפָּט שָׁלוֹם שִׁפְטוּ בְּשַׁעֲרֵיכֶם."

18. עַל הָאֱמֶת וְעַל הַדִּין וְעַל הַשָּׁלוֹם — Because of truth; because of justice; and because of peace.

The Talmud (*Yerushalmi Ta'anis* 4:2) explains that all three are really one. When people know that the courts of justice will uncover their false claims, they will be afraid to lie. In this way justice brings truth. And once there is justice and truth, all arguments will be ended and there will be peace. That is what the *Navi* Zechariah teaches us, "[When there is] truth and justice, [then] peace shall rule in your gates."

❧ CHAPTER TWO / פרק שני ❧

1. [R]abbi [Yehudah *Hanassi*] taught: (a) What is the proper path for a person to choose for himself? He should choose a path that is good for himself and causes other people to admire him. (b) Be just as careful in doing a *mitzvah* that you think is not important as you are in doing a *mitzvah* that you think is important, because you do not know which *mitzvah* will earn you a greater reward. (c) Compare the amount you spend doing a *mitzvah* with the reward you will receive for doing it; and compare the amount you gain by doing a sin with the punishment you will receive for doing it.

(d) Think of three things and you will not sin. Know that these three things are above you: An Eye is watching you; an Ear is listening to you; and whatever you say or do is written in a Book.

2. Rabban Gamliel the son of R' Yehudah *Hanassi* taught: (a) It is good to combine Torah study with a job, for working hard at both of them stops a person from sinning. Even more, any Torah study that is not combined with a job may end up as nothing and may even lead to sin.

(b) When you work for the community, you should work for *Hashem's* sake, then the good deeds of your fathers will help you, for their good deeds last forever. And even though you were helped by their good deeds, *Hashem* will still reward you as if you did everything by yourself.

[א] **רַבִּי** אוֹמֵר: אֵיזוֹ הִיא דֶרֶךְ יְשָׁרָה שֶׁיָּבֹר לוֹ הָאָדָם? כָּל שֶׁהִיא תִפְאֶרֶת לְעֹשֶׂהָ וְתִפְאֶרֶת לוֹ מִן הָאָדָם. וֶהֱוֵי זָהִיר בְּמִצְוָה קַלָּה כְּבַחֲמוּרָה, שֶׁאֵין אַתָּה יוֹדֵעַ מַתַּן שְׂכָרָן שֶׁל מִצְוֹת. וֶהֱוֵי מְחַשֵּׁב הֶפְסֵד מִצְוָה כְּנֶגֶד שְׂכָרָהּ, וּשְׂכַר עֲבֵרָה כְּנֶגֶד הֶפְסֵדָהּ.

הִסְתַּכֵּל בִּשְׁלֹשָׁה דְבָרִים, וְאֵין אַתָּה בָא לִידֵי עֲבֵרָה: דַּע מַה לְמַעְלָה מִמְּךָ: עַיִן רוֹאָה, וְאֹזֶן שׁוֹמַעַת; וְכָל מַעֲשֶׂיךָ בַּסֵּפֶר נִכְתָּבִים.

[ב] רַבָּן גַּמְלִיאֵל בְּנוֹ שֶׁל רַבִּי יְהוּדָה הַנָּשִׂיא אוֹמֵר: יָפֶה תַלְמוּד תּוֹרָה עִם דֶּרֶךְ אֶרֶץ, שֶׁיְּגִיעַת שְׁנֵיהֶם מַשְׁכַּחַת עָוֹן. וְכָל תּוֹרָה שֶׁאֵין עִמָּהּ מְלָאכָה, סוֹפָהּ בְּטֵלָה וְגוֹרֶרֶת עָוֹן.

וְכָל הָעוֹסְקִים עִם הַצִּבּוּר, יִהְיוּ עוֹסְקִים עִמָּהֶם לְשֵׁם שָׁמַיִם, שֶׁזְּכוּת אֲבוֹתָם מְסַיַּעְתָּם, וְצִדְקָתָם עוֹמֶדֶת לָעַד. וְאַתֶּם, מַעֲלֶה אֲנִי עֲלֵיכֶם שָׂכָר הַרְבֵּה כְּאִלּוּ עֲשִׂיתֶם.

1. תִּפְאֶרֶת לְעֹשֶׂהָ וְתִפְאֶרֶת לוֹ מִן הָאָדָם — **That is good for him and causes other people to like him.**

Most of the *middos* have opposites and in-betweens. For every *middah*, we must try to follow the in-between path. Let us take spending money as an example. Some people spend or give away every dollar they earn. They are called spendthrifts. Other people do just the opposite. They save as much money as they can, almost never give charity, and buy only what they absolutely must. These people are called misers.

Everyone likes a spendthrift. He's a good customer, so the shopkeepers like him. He gives away a lot, so the poor like him. He buys his friends presents, so they like him. He eats expensive meals, so the restaurant owner likes him. But all this spending is not good for himself. Soon he will have no more money to buy the things he needs.

A miser is just the opposite. Nobody likes him. He's not a good customer; he never gives charity; he never buys presents; and he eats very, very little. Yet, in a selfish way, he is doing good for himself. Since he saves all his money, he is very likely to become rich.

In between the miser and the spendthrift is the person who spends as much as he has to, and gives as much charity as he can afford. But still he makes sure to save enough money in case of an emergency. This person acts with נְדִיבוּת, *generosity*. He follows "a path that is good for himself and causes other people to admire him."

עַיִן רוֹאָה וְאֹזֶן שׁוֹמַעַת וְכָל מַעֲשֶׂיךָ בַּסֵּפֶר נִכְתָּבִים — **An Eye is watching you; an Ear is listening to you; and whatever you say or do is written in a Book.**

Many years ago, before the invention of cameras and tape recorders, it was very difficult to understand this *mishnah*. But today we can see things happening in front of us on film, even though they really took place many years ago. And we can hear recordings of things said a long time ago.

The Eye, Ear and Book of our *mishnah* all refer to *Hashem*. He sees and hears everything, and never forgets anything. It is as if a camera and a microphone are recording whatever you do and storing your actions and words on film and tapes.

It is good to combine Torah study with a job.

2. וְכָל תּוֹרָה שֶׁאֵין עִמָּהּ מְלָאכָה סוֹפָהּ בְּטֵלָה וְגוֹרֶרֶת עָוֹן — Any Torah study that is not combined with a job may end up as nothing and may even lead to sin.

The words דֶּרֶךְ אֶרֶץ and מְלָאכָה are translated ''job''. But they really mean a way of earning money for himself and his family. A man must provide his family with food, clothing and a place to live. Most people have to spend a good part of their day at their jobs in order to support themselves. Some people do not have to work at a job because they have saved up enough money to supply their needs. Others are supported by relatives or by a Kollel. They can spend their entire day studying Torah even if they don't have a job.

But if someone has nobody to support him and he does not support himself, his family will soon be hungry and their clothing will be ragged. He will not be able to continue his studies. And he may even turn dishonest in order to supply his family's needs.

3. (c) Be careful of government officials, for they become friends with a person only for their own good. They act friendly when it is good for them, but they do not help someone when he needs help.

[ג] הֱווּ זְהִירִין בָּרָשׁוּת, שֶׁאֵין מְקָרְבִין לוֹ לְאָדָם אֶלָּא לְצֹרֶךְ עַצְמָן. נִרְאִין כְּאוֹהֲבִין בִּשְׁעַת הֲנָאָתָן, וְאֵין עוֹמְדִין לוֹ לְאָדָם בִּשְׁעַת דָּחֳקוֹ.

4. He also used to teach:

Fulfill *Hashem's mitzvos* as you fulfill own desires, then *Hashem* will fulfill your desires as if they were His own.

Destroy your own desires when they are different from *Hashem's*, then *Hashem* will destroy the desires of others when they are different from yours.

[ד] הוּא הָיָה אוֹמֵר: עֲשֵׂה רְצוֹנוֹ כִּרְצוֹנֶךָ, כְּדֵי שֶׁיַּעֲשֶׂה רְצוֹנְךָ כִּרְצוֹנוֹ.

בַּטֵּל רְצוֹנְךָ מִפְּנֵי רְצוֹנוֹ, כְּדֵי שֶׁיְּבַטֵּל רְצוֹן אֲחֵרִים מִפְּנֵי רְצוֹנֶךָ.

5. Hillel taught: (a) Do not separate yourself from the community. (b) As long as you live, do not think that you will never sin. (c) Do not judge another person until you are in his place. (d) Keep your private thoughts to yourself, even if you think nobody else is listening, because in the end what you say will be heard by others. (e) Do not say, "I will study when I have free time," for you may never have free time.

6. He used to teach: (a) A fool cannot be afraid of sin. (b) A person who has not studied Torah cannot be very careful about mitzvos. (c) A person who is too shy to ask questions cannot learn. (d) A person who gets angry easily cannot teach. (e) A person who spends too much time in business cannot become a Torah scholar. (f) In a place where there are no leaders, try to be a leader.

7. Hillel once saw a skull floating on the water. He said to the skull, "Because you drowned others, you were drowned. And those who drowned you will also be drowned."

[ה] הִלֵּל אוֹמֵר: אַל תִּפְרוֹשׁ מִן הַצִּבּוּר. וְאַל תַּאֲמִין בְּעַצְמְךָ עַד יוֹם מוֹתְךָ. וְאַל תָּדִין אֶת חֲבֵרְךָ עַד שֶׁתַּגִּיעַ לִמְקוֹמוֹ. וְאַל תֹּאמַר דָּבָר שֶׁאִי אֶפְשָׁר לִשְׁמוֹעַ, שֶׁסּוֹפוֹ לְהִשָּׁמַע. וְאַל תֹּאמַר לִכְשֶׁאֶפָּנֶה אֶשְׁנֶה, שֶׁמָּא לֹא תִפָּנֶה.

[ו] הוּא הָיָה אוֹמֵר: אֵין בּוּר יְרֵא חֵטְא. וְלֹא עַם הָאָרֶץ חָסִיד. וְלֹא הַבַּיְשָׁן לָמֵד. וְלֹא הַקַּפְּדָן מְלַמֵּד. וְלֹא כָּל הַמַּרְבֶּה בִסְחוֹרָה מַחְכִּים. וּבִמְקוֹם שֶׁאֵין אֲנָשִׁים הִשְׁתַּדֵּל לִהְיוֹת אִישׁ.

[ז] אַף הוּא רָאָה גֻּלְגֹּלֶת אַחַת שֶׁצָּפָה עַל פְּנֵי הַמָּיִם. אָמַר לָהּ, "עַל דְּאַטֵּפְתְּ אַטְפוּךְ. וְסוֹף מְטַיְּפָיִךְ יְטוּפוּן."

---

5. אַל תִּפְרוֹשׁ מִן הַצִּבּוּר — **Do not separate yourself from the community.**

When trouble strikes the community, everyone must join in the sorrow. For example, if a row of houses is destroyed by fire, the family whose home remained standing should not say, "Well, that's their problem, not ours." Instead, they should feel just as sorrowful as if their own home was burned. And they should offer as much help as possible to the unfortunate ones.

וְאַל תַּאֲמִין בְּעַצְמְךָ עַד יוֹם מוֹתְךָ — **As long as you live, do not think that you will never sin.**

Nobody can ever know for sure that his *yetzer hara* will never lead him to sin. The *Gemara* (*Berachos* 29a) tells us the story of Yochanan who was the *Kohein Gadol* (High Priest) for eighty years. Yet, at the end of his life, he became a sinner. So we see that everybody must always be on guard against his *yetzer hara*.

וְאַל תָּדִין אֶת חֲבֵרְךָ עַד שֶׁתַּגִּיעַ לִמְקוֹמוֹ — **Do not judge another person until you are in his place.**

When we see our friend doing the wrong thing, we should not call him "wicked" or "bad." Maybe if we were in the same situation we would act in an even worse way. Instead of judging our friend, we should remind him in a nice way that what he is doing is wrong.

שֶׁסּוֹפוֹ לְהִשָּׁמַע — **Because, in the end, what you say will be heard.**

Shlomo *Hamelech* (King Solomon) taught: "Even in your thoughts do not curse a king; even in your private bedroom,

do not curse a wise man; for the birds in the sky will carry your voice, and the winged creatures will repeat your words" (*Koheles* 10:20).

6. וְלֹא עַם הָאָרֶץ חָסִיד — **A person who has not studied Torah cannot be very careful about mitzvos.**

Some people think that they can do all the *mitzvos* even if they don't spend any time studying the Torah. But they are wrong. If someone does not learn Torah, he will not know how to do the *mitzvos* correctly.

וְלֹא הַקַּפְּדָן מְלַמֵּד — **A person who gets angry easily cannot teach.**

If a teacher does not have patience with his students, they will be afraid to ask questions. And as the *Mishnah* just said, "A person who doesn't ask questions cannot learn."

7. עַל דְּאַטֵּפְתְּ אַטְפוּךְ וְסוֹף מְטַיְּפָיִךְ יְטוּפוּן — **Because you drowned others, you were drowned; and those who drowned you will also be drowned.**

Nothing happens without a reason. *Hashem* punishes sinfulness מִדָּה כְּנֶגֶד מִדָּה, measure for measure. In other words, the punishment always fits the crime. When something bad happens, the victim should examine his deeds. Perhaps he did something wrong and is being punished. Of course his sore throat was caused by germs. But perhaps these germs would not have entered his throat, if he had not spoken *lashon hara,* bad about others.

In the same way, if a person was the victim of a crime, he should consider it as a punishment for some sin that he did. But at the same time, he should not think that his attacker will escape without punishment.

8. He used to teach that too much of certain things are not good for a person: (a) The more flesh, the more worms; (b) the more property, the more problems; (c) the more wives, the more witchcraft; (d) the more maids, the more sins; (e) the more servants, the more stealing.

But about other things he taught that the more you have the better it is: (a) The more Torah, the more life; (b) the more study, the more wisdom; (c) the more advice, the more understanding; (d) the more charity, the more peace.

If a person has gained a good name, he has gained something good for himself. If a person has gained Torah knowledge, he has gained himself life in the World to Come.

9. Rabban Yochanan ben Zakkai learned Torah from Hillel and Shammai. He taught:

Even if you have studied a lot of Torah, do not be boastful, for that is what you were created to do.

10. Rabban Yochanan ben Zakkai had five main students. They were R' Eliezer ben Hyrkanos, R' Yehoshua ben Chanania, R' Yose the *Kohein*, R' Shimon ben Nesanel and R' Elazar ben Arach.

11. He used to praise each of his students:

[ח] הוּא הָיָה אוֹמֵר: מַרְבֶּה בָשָׂר, מַרְבֶּה רִמָּה; מַרְבֶּה נְכָסִים, מַרְבֶּה דְאָגָה; מַרְבֶּה נָשִׁים, מַרְבֶּה כְשָׁפִים; מַרְבֶּה שְׁפָחוֹת, מַרְבֶּה זִמָּה; מַרְבֶּה עֲבָדִים, מַרְבֶּה גָזֵל.

מַרְבֶּה תוֹרָה, מַרְבֶּה חַיִּים; מַרְבֶּה יְשִׁיבָה, מַרְבֶּה חָכְמָה; מַרְבֶּה עֵצָה, מַרְבֶּה תְבוּנָה; מַרְבֶּה צְדָקָה, מַרְבֶּה שָׁלוֹם. קָנָה שֵׁם טוֹב, קָנָה לְעַצְמוֹ. קָנָה לוֹ דִבְרֵי תוֹרָה, קָנָה לוֹ חַיֵּי הָעוֹלָם הַבָּא.

[ט] רַבָּן יוֹחָנָן בֶּן זַכַּאי קִבֵּל מֵהִלֵּל וּמִשַּׁמַּאי. הוּא הָיָה אוֹמֵר: אִם לָמַדְתָּ תוֹרָה הַרְבֵּה, אַל תַּחֲזִיק טוֹבָה לְעַצְמְךָ, כִּי לְכָךְ נוֹצָרְתָּ.

[י] חֲמִשָּׁה תַלְמִידִים הָיוּ לוֹ לְרַבָּן יוֹחָנָן בֶּן זַכַּאי, וְאֵלּוּ הֵן: רַבִּי אֱלִיעֶזֶר בֶּן הֻרְקָנוֹס, רַבִּי יְהוֹשֻׁעַ בֶּן חֲנַנְיָא, רַבִּי יוֹסֵי הַכֹּהֵן, רַבִּי שִׁמְעוֹן בֶּן נְתַנְאֵל, וְרַבִּי אֶלְעָזָר בֶּן עֲרָךְ.

[יא] הוּא הָיָה מוֹנֶה שִׁבְחָן:

---

8. מַרְבֶּה בָשָׂר מַרְבֶּה רִמָּה — The more flesh, the more worms.
People who stuff themselves on heavy, fatty foods may get pleasure from their meals and may satisfy their huge appetites. But fat people are more likely to get sick than thin people. The more flesh a person has, the more chance he has of becoming sick with the "worms" of disease.

מַרְבֶּה נָשִׁים מַרְבֶּה כְשָׁפִים — The more wives, the more witchcraft.
In olden times, a man was allowed to marry many wives. Often the wives would be jealous of one another and this would cause a lot of trouble. In fact, when a man had more than one wife, each wife was called a צָרָה (trouble) to the others. Sometimes one wife's jealousy would cause her to try anything — even witchcraft — to become her husband's favorite wife.

מַרְבֶּה שְׁפָחוֹת מַרְבֶּה זִמָּה; מַרְבֶּה עֲבָדִים מַרְבֶּה גָזֵל — The more maids, the more sins; the more servants, the more stealing.
Rich people used to have slaves and maids working in their homes. These servants did not care to follow the laws of the Torah. The Sages did not think this was a good idea. Here we learn that if there are many such servants and maids in someone's house, that house will soon be full of stealing and other sins.

9. כִּי לְכָךְ נוֹצָרְתָּ — For that is what you were created to do.
Birds were created with wings so that they could fly. Fish were created with fins so that they could swim. Can a bird boast to a fish, "I can travel through the sky!"? Can a fish boast to a bird, "I can swim under the sea!"? Of course not. They are only doing what they were created to do.

People were created with intelligence and understanding so that they could study *Hashem's* Torah. Can a person boast, "I have learned much Torah!"? Of course not. He is only doing what he was created to do.

10. חֲמִשָּׁה תַלְמִידִים — Five main students.
This *mishnah* seems to teach us very little. It is just a list of the names of five people! But really we can improve ourselves very much by just mentioning the names of these *tzaddikim*. For their names remind us of them, and thinking of them reminds us of what they did and what they taught. And these lessons help us to become better people. That is why Shlomo *Hamelech* taught us, זֵכֶר צַדִּיק לִבְרָכָה, Mentioning a *tzaddik's* name is a blessing (*Mishlei* 10:7).

11. הוּא הָיָה מוֹנֶה שִׁבְחָן — He used to praise each of his students.
We learned in the last *mishnah* that just mentioning a *tzaddik's* name will make us better people. Certainly when

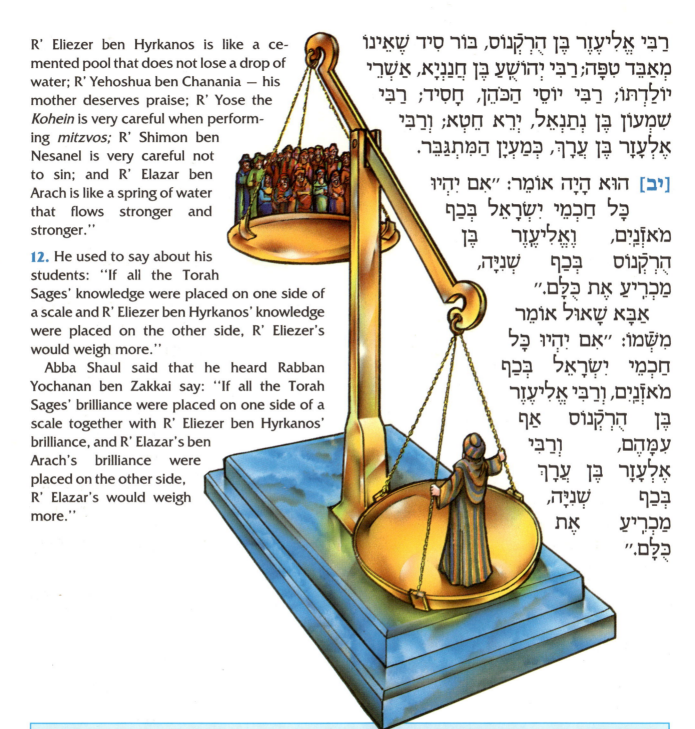

R' Eliezer ben Hyrkanos is like a cemented pool that does not lose a drop of water; R' Yehoshua ben Chanania — his mother deserves praise; R' Yose the *Kohein* is very careful when performing *mitzvos*; R' Shimon ben Nesanel is very careful not to sin; and R' Elazar ben Arach is like a spring of water that flows stronger and stronger.''

12. He used to say about his students: "If all the Torah Sages' knowledge were placed on one side of a scale and R' Eliezer ben Hyrkanos' knowledge were placed on the other side, R' Eliezer's would weigh more.''

Abba Shaul said that he heard Rabban Yochanan ben Zakkai say: "If all the Torah Sages' brilliance were placed on one side of a scale together with R' Eliezer ben Hyrkanos' brilliance, and R' Elazar's ben Arach's brilliance were placed on the other side, R' Elazar's would weigh more.''

רַבִּי אֱלִיעֶזֶר בֶּן הֻרְקָנוֹס, בּוֹר סִיד שֶׁאֵינוֹ מְאַבֵּד טִפָּה; רַבִּי יְהוֹשֻׁעַ בֶּן חֲנַנְיָא, אַשְׁרֵי יוֹלַדְתּוֹ; רַבִּי יוֹסֵי הַכֹּהֵן, חָסִיד; רַבִּי שִׁמְעוֹן בֶּן נְתַנְאֵל, יְרֵא חֵטְא, וְרַבִּי אֶלְעָזָר בֶּן עֲרָךְ, כְּמַעְיָן הַמִּתְגַּבֵּר.

[יב] הוּא הָיָה אוֹמֵר: ''אִם יִהְיוּ כָּל חַכְמֵי יִשְׂרָאֵל בְּכַף מֹאזְנַיִם, וֶאֱלִיעֶזֶר בֶּן הֻרְקָנוֹס בְּכַף שְׁנִיָּה, מַכְרִיעַ אֶת כֻּלָּם.'' אַבָּא שָׁאוּל אוֹמֵר מִשְּׁמוֹ: ''אִם יִהְיוּ כָּל חַכְמֵי יִשְׂרָאֵל בְּכַף מֹאזְנַיִם, וְרַבִּי אֱלִיעֶזֶר בֶּן הֻרְקָנוֹס אַף עִמָּהֶם, וְרַבִּי אֶלְעָזָר בֶּן עֲרָךְ בְּכַף שְׁנִיָּה, מַכְרִיעַ אֶת כֻּלָּם.''

we describe how great these *tzaddikim* were, we learn even more.

שֶׁאֵינוֹ מְאַבֵּד טִפָּה — That does not lose a drop of water.
Torah is compared to fresh water. R' Eliezer ben Hyrkanos never forgot what he had learned. Therefore he was like a leakproof tank that never loses a drop of water.

אַשְׁרֵי יוֹלַדְתּוֹ — His mother deserves praise. Before her son was born, R' Yehoshua's mother would go to every *beis midrash* (study hall) in her city. There, she would ask the rabbis to pray that her child would be a Torah scholar.

After he was born, she would bring his cradle to the *beis*

midrash. She wanted him to become used to the sounds of Torah study, even before he could understand them.

חָסִיד — Very careful when performing *mitzvos*.
A חָסִיד, *chassid*, is a person who is so careful when performing *mitzvos* that he will usually do much more than the Torah demands of him.

כְּמַעְיָן הַמִּתְגַּבֵּר — Like a spring of water that flows stronger and stronger.
R' Elazar remembered whatever he had learned. And he kept adding more and more original explanations to what his teachers had taught him.

13. Rabban Yochanan ben Zakkai told his students, "Go out and see if you can discover which good path each person should follow."

R' Eliezer said, "Look at everything with a good eye."

[**יג**] אָמַר לָהֶם: צְאוּ וּרְאוּ אֵיזוֹ הִיא דֶּרֶךְ טוֹבָה שֶׁיִּדְבַּק בָּהּ הָאָדָם.

רַבִּי אֱלִיעֶזֶר אוֹמֵר: עַיִן טוֹבָה.

R' Yehoshua said, "A good friend."

R' Yose said, "A good neighbor."

R' Shimon said, "Before you do something, think of what it will lead to."

R' Elazar said, "Have a good heart."

Rabban Yochanan then said, "I like Elazar ben Arach's answer better than the others answers, because 'a good heart' contains everything that all of you have said."

14. He then told his students, "Go out and see if you can discover which evil path each person should keep away from."

R' Eliezer said, "Don't look at anything with a bad eye."

R' Yehoshua said, "Don't be a bad friend."

R' Yose said, "Don't be a bad neighbor."

R' Shimon said, "Don't be a person who borrows and then doesn't pay back. Borrowing from another person is like borrowing from Hashem. And we are taught in *Tehillim* (37:21): "A wicked person borrows and does not pay back, but *Hashem* is a *Tzaddik,* He is kind and He gives."

R' Elazar said, "Don't have an evil heart."

Rabban Yochanan then said, "I like Elazar ben Arach's answer better than the other answers, because 'an evil heart' contains everything that all of you have said."

15. Each of Rabban Yochanan's students taught three important lessons. R' Eliezer taught: (a) Your friend's honor should be as important to you as your own, therefore you should not get angry easily. (b) Do *teshuvah* for your sins the day before you die. (c) Warm

רַבִּי יְהוֹשֻׁעַ אוֹמֵר: חָבֵר טוֹב.

רַבִּי יוֹסֵי אוֹמֵר: שָׁכֵן טוֹב.

רַבִּי שִׁמְעוֹן אוֹמֵר: הָרוֹאֶה אֶת הַנּוֹלָד.

רַבִּי אֶלְעָזָר אוֹמֵר: לֵב טוֹב.

אָמַר לָהֶם: רוֹאֶה אֲנִי אֶת דִּבְרֵי אֶלְעָזָר בֶּן עֲרָךְ מִדִּבְרֵיכֶם, שֶׁבִּכְלָל דְּבָרָיו דִּבְרֵיכֶם.

[יד] אָמַר לָהֶם: צְאוּ וּרְאוּ אֵיזוֹ הִיא דֶרֶךְ רָעָה שֶׁיִּתְרַחֵק מִמֶּנָּה הָאָדָם.

רַבִּי אֱלִיעֶזֶר אוֹמֵר: עַיִן רָעָה.

רַבִּי יְהוֹשֻׁעַ אוֹמֵר: חָבֵר רָע.

רַבִּי יוֹסֵי אוֹמֵר: שָׁכֵן רָע.

רַבִּי שִׁמְעוֹן אוֹמֵר: הַלֹּוֶה וְאֵינוֹ מְשַׁלֵּם. אֶחָד הַלֹּוֶה מִן הָאָדָם כְּלֹוֶה מִן הַמָּקוֹם, שֶׁנֶּאֱמַר: "לֹוֶה רָשָׁע וְלֹא יְשַׁלֵּם, וְצַדִּיק חוֹנֵן וְנוֹתֵן."

רַבִּי אֶלְעָזָר אוֹמֵר: לֵב רָע.

אָמַר לָהֶם: רוֹאֶה אֲנִי אֶת דִּבְרֵי אֶלְעָזָר בֶּן עֲרָךְ מִדִּבְרֵיכֶם, שֶׁבִּכְלָל דְּבָרָיו דִּבְרֵיכֶם.

[טו] הֵם אָמְרוּ שְׁלשָׁה דְבָרִים. רַבִּי אֱלִיעֶזֶר אוֹמֵר: יְהִי כְבוֹד חֲבֵרְךָ חָבִיב עָלֶיךָ כְּשֶׁלָּךְ, וְאַל תְּהִי נוֹחַ לִכְעוֹס; וְשׁוּב יוֹם אֶחָד לִפְנֵי מִיתָתְךָ; וֶהֱוֵי

13. חָבֵר טוֹב . . . שָׁכֵן טוֹב — A good friend ... A good neighbor.

These lessons tell us to choose our friends and neighbors carefully. We learn good things from good people. We learn bad things from bad people. Another thing that these lessons teach is that we must always try to be good friends and good neighbors.

14. לֹוֶה רָשָׁע וְלֹא יְשַׁלֵּם וְצַדִּיק חוֹנֵן וְנוֹתֵן — A wicked person borrows and does not pay back, but Hashem is a Tzaddik, He is kind and he gives.

When a wicked man borrows money, he has no intention of ever returning it. But *Hashem* does not want the good lender to lose his money, so He finds a way to return the money. In this way, if a person borrows and does not try to

return what he borrowed, it is as if he took money from *Hashem*.

15. וְשׁוּב — Do teshuvah.

Doing *teshuvah* means telling *Hashem* that we are sorry for the sins that we have done, and promising not to repeat them. It also means apologizing to the people whom we have treated badly, and asking them to forgive us.

וְשׁוּב יוֹם אֶחָד לִפְנֵי מִיתָתְךָ — Do teshuvah for your sins the day before you die.

When R' Eliezer taught this lesson to his students, they asked him, "But does a person know on which day he will die?"

R' Eliezer answered, "Therefore he must do *teshuvah* every day, for maybe he will die on the next day."

your soul with the fiery words of the Torah Sages, but be careful not to burn yourself with their coals; for their words can bite like a fox, sting like a scorpion, and hiss like a serpent — in fact, all their words are like burning coals.

16. R' Yehoshua taught that three bad things remove a person from this world: A bad eye; the *yetzer hara;* and hating other people.

17. R' Yose taught: (a) Your friend's money should be as important to you as your own. (b) You must prepare yourself to study Torah because you do not learn it by inheritance. (c) Everything you do must be done for *Hashem's* sake.

18. R' Shimon taught: (a) Be very careful about when to recite *Shema* and *Shemoneh Esrei.*

מִתְחַמֵּם כְּנֶגֶד אוּרָן שֶׁל חֲכָמִים, וֶהֱוֵי זָהִיר בְּגַחַלְתָּן שֶׁלֹּא תִכָּוֶה — שֶׁנְּשִׁיכָתָן נְשִׁיכַת שׁוּעָל, וַעֲקִיצָתָן עֲקִיצַת עַקְרָב, וּלְחִישָׁתָן לְחִישַׁת שָׂרָף, וְכָל דִּבְרֵיהֶם כְּגַחֲלֵי אֵשׁ.

[טז] רַבִּי יְהוֹשֻׁעַ אוֹמֵר: עַיִן הָרָע, וְיֵצֶר הָרָע, וְשִׂנְאַת הַבְּרִיּוֹת מוֹצִיאִין אֶת הָאָדָם מִן הָעוֹלָם.

[יז] רַבִּי יוֹסֵי אוֹמֵר: יְהִי מָמוֹן חֲבֵרְךָ חָבִיב עָלֶיךָ כְּשֶׁלָּךְ; וְהַתְקֵן עַצְמְךָ לִלְמוֹד תּוֹרָה, שֶׁאֵינָהּ יְרֻשָּׁה לָךְ; וְכָל מַעֲשֶׂיךָ יִהְיוּ לְשֵׁם שָׁמָיִם.

[יח] רַבִּי שִׁמְעוֹן אוֹמֵר: הֱוֵי זָהִיר בִּקְרִיאַת שְׁמַע וּבִתְפִלָּה;

וֶהֱוֵי מִתְחַמֵּם כְּנֶגֶד אוּרָן שֶׁל חֲכָמִים — **Warm your soul with the fiery words of the Torah Sages.**

We should always try to keep close to those who are well learned in Torah. We will hear many good things from them and we will also learn by watching what they do. But we must always be careful to show them great respect and to act properly in their presence. Otherwise they may "burn" us with "flaming" words of *mussar* (rebuke).

16. עַיִן הָרָע וְיֵצֶר הָרָע וְשִׂנְאַת הַבְּרִיּוֹת — **A bad eye; the yetzer hara; and hate for other people.**

"A bad eye" means being jealous of others. "Yetzer hara" means the desire and appetite for things that the Torah tells us not to do. And "hating other people" is caused by a sickness called depression. Someone who is depressed thinks that people don't care about him. So he starts to hate them in return. He will soon begin to hate even himself and will stop taking care of his needs. Jealousy, desire and depression are three bad things that don't allow a person to live a peaceful life.

17. שֶׁאֵינָהּ יְרֻשָּׁה לָךְ — **You do not learn it by inheritance.**

A *Kohein's* son is a *Kohein,* even though he does nothing to earn this position. A rich man's son may be rich, even though he never worked for a penny in his whole life. But a wise man's son will not become wise unless he spends time and makes an effort to gain wisdom. No matter how much Torah a father studies, no matter how much knowledge he gathers, his sons will not inherit his knowledge, they will not become Torah scholars — unless they prepare themselves with Torah study.

18. הֱוֵי זָהִיר בִּקְרִיאַת שְׁמַע וּבִתְפִלָּה — **Be very careful about when to recite Shema and Shemoneh Esrei.**

Certain *mitzvos* may be done at any time during the day. If one forgets to do them in the morning, he may still do

(b) When you pray, do not pray out of habit, but beg for kindness and mercy from *Hashem*; as the *Navi* (*Yoel* 2:13) teaches, "He is merciful and kind, slow to anger, full of love and forgiving of evil." (c) Do not think of yourself as an evil person.

19. R' Elazar taught:

(a) Put much effort into the study of Torah. (b) Know what to answer to a person who makes fun of the Torah. (c) Know who your Master is; and that He can be trusted to pay you for your work.

20. R' Tarfon taught:

The day is short; the job is big; the workers are lazy; the reward is great; and the Master is demanding.

21. He also taught:

(a) You are not expected to finish the job, but you are not free to quit. (b) If you have learned much Torah, you will be given a great reward. (c) Your Master can be trusted to pay you for your work. (d) You should know that a *tzaddik* receives his reward in the World to Come.

וּכְשֶׁאַתָּה מִתְפַּלֵל, אַל תַּעַשׂ תְּפִלָּתְךָ קֶבַע, אֶלָּא רַחֲמִים וְתַחֲנוּנִים לִפְנֵי הַמָּקוֹם, שֶׁנֶּאֱמַר: "כִּי חַנּוּן וְרַחוּם הוּא אֶרֶךְ אַפַּיִם וְרַב חֶסֶד וְנִחָם עַל הָרָעָה." וְאַל תְּהִי רָשָׁע בִּפְנֵי עַצְמֶךָ.

[יט] רַבִּי אֶלְעָזָר אוֹמֵר: הֱוֵי שָׁקוּד לִלְמוֹד תּוֹרָה. וְדַע מַה שֶׁתָּשִׁיב לְאֶפִּיקוֹרוֹס. וְדַע לִפְנֵי מִי אַתָּה עָמֵל; וְנֶאֱמָן הוּא בַּעַל מְלַאכְתְּךָ, שֶׁיְשַׁלֶּם לְךָ שְׂכַר פְּעֻלָתֶךָ.

[כ] רַבִּי טַרְפוֹן אוֹמֵר: הַיּוֹם קָצֵר; וְהַמְּלָאכָה מְרֻבָּה; וְהַפּוֹעֲלִים עֲצֵלִים, וְהַשָּׂכָר הַרְבֵּה; וּבַעַל הַבַּיִת דּוֹחֵק.

[כא] הוּא הָיָה אוֹמֵר: לֹא עָלֶיךָ הַמְּלָאכָה לִגְמוֹר, וְלֹא אַתָּה בֶן חֹרִין לְהִבָּטֵל מִמֶּנָּה. אִם לָמַדְתָּ תּוֹרָה הַרְבֵּה, נוֹתְנִים לְךָ שָׂכָר הַרְבֵּה. וְנֶאֱמָן הוּא בַּעַל מְלַאכְתְּךָ, שֶׁיְשַׁלֶּם לְךָ שְׂכַר פְּעֻלָתֶךָ. וְדַע שֶׁמַּתַּן שְׂכָרָן שֶׁל צַדִּיקִים לֶעָתִיד לָבֹא.

---

them in the afternoon. For example, on Purim the *Megillah* must be read once at night and a second time in the morning. If someone did not read (or hear) the *Megillah* early on Purim morning, he may still read it in the afternoon.

But with *Shema* and *Shemoneh Esrei* this is not true. The morning *Shema* must be recited during the first three hours of the day. *Shemoneh Esrei* of *Shacharis* must be recited during the first four hours of the day. Once that time has passed, the *mitzvah* of reciting these prayers at their proper time is lost.

וְאַל תְּהִי רָשָׁע בִּפְנֵי עַצְמֶךָ — Do not think of yourself as an evil person.

Even if someone has sinned many times, he should not think of himself as an evil person. If he thinks of himself as an evil person, he will give up trying to change his ways. He will just get worse and worse. Instead, he should admit that he has done wrong and try to mend his ways. If he thinks of himself as a good person who has made a mistake, he will want to improve himself. And he will succeed.

19. וְדַע מַה שֶׁתָּשִׁיב לְאֶפִּיקוֹרוֹס — Know what to answer to a person who makes fun of the Torah.

Notice that the *mishnah* does not say, "Know what to tell," or, "Know what to ask." When it comes to people who

make fun of the Torah, we should keep our distance. We should not start any conversations or arguments with them. However, if they ask us questions, we must be prepared to answer them.

20. הַיּוֹם . . . וְהַמְּלָאכָה . . . — The day . . . the job . . .

"The day" stands for life in this world, which is very short compared to the life in *Olam Haba* (the World to Come).

"The job" is gaining as much knowledge of the Torah and serving *Hashem* by doing His *mitzvos*. It is a big job, for the Torah is endless and the *mitzvos* are many. "The workers," all of us, are lazy when it comes to fulfilling our job. But we must always remember that "the reward" — life in *Olam Haba* — is greater than our greatest dream. And the "Master," *Hashem*, demands that we do our job as best as we can.

21. לֹא עָלֶיךָ הַמְּלָאכָה לִגְמוֹר — You are not expected to finish the job.

As we learned in the last *mishnah*, the job is very big. But even though *Hashem* demands that we do our jobs as best as we can, He does not expect us to complete our jobs. Just the same, we are not free to quit in the middle, but must continue to do our best for as long as we are able.

1. Akavia ben Mehalalel taught:
Always think about three things, and you will not sin. The three things are:
(a) From where did you come?
(b) To where are you going?
(c) Before whom will you have to explain all of your actions?

[א] עֲקַבְיָא בֶּן מַהֲלַלְאֵל אוֹמֵר: הִסְתַּכֵּל בִּשְׁלֹשָׁה דְבָרִים וְאֵין אַתָּה בָא לִידֵי עֲבֵרָה. דַּע – מֵאַיִן בָּאתָ? וּלְאָן אַתָּה הוֹלֵךְ? וְלִפְנֵי מִי אַתָּה עָתִיד לִתֵּן דִּין וְחֶשְׁבּוֹן?

From where did you come? To where are you going?

1. הִסְתַּכֵּל בִּשְׁלֹשָׁה דְבָרִים — **Always think about three things.**

There are three *middos* that cause a person to become sinful. One of these three is גַּאֲוָה, *pride*. A person with too much pride seeks honor and glory for himself. He will do whatever he can to feed his pride — he might even sin.

The second of the three *middos* that lead to sinfulness is תַּאֲוָה, *desire*, a never-satisfied appetite for the most, the biggest, the fanciest, the finest of everything. A person who does not control his desires will do anything to get more and more — he might even steal.

The third of the *middos* that leads to sinfulness is אֶפִּיקוֹרְסוּת, *not believing in Hashem*. If a person puts Hashem out of his mind, nothing will stop him from doing whatever he wants to do. But a person with love and fear of Hashem will always think twice before doing anything. His love of Hashem will cause him to ask, "Is this what Hashem wants me to do? Will what I am doing make Hashem proud of me?" If this doesn't stop him from sinning, then his fear of Hashem will make him think, "If I do something bad, Hashem will punish me."

This *mishnah* tells us how we can keep away the three bad *middos* of אֶפִּיקוֹרְסוּת and גַּאֲוָה, תַּאֲוָה.

The answers to these questions are:

(a) From where did you come? — From a tiny cell that could have easily spoiled.

(b) To where are you going? — To a place of dust, where even tiny worms are stronger than the strongest man.

(c) Before Whom will you have to explain all of your actions? — Before *Hashem*, the King of kings, He is the Holy One, Blessed is He.

2. R' Chanina the assistant *Kohein Gadol* taught:

Pray for the peace of the government, because if people were not afraid of the government, they would swallow each other alive.

3. R' Chanina ben Teradyon taught:

If two people sit together and do not speak any words of Torah, they are like a group of jokers — as it is written in *Tehillim* (1:1-2), "He did not sit in a 'group of jokers,' but he desired *Hashem's* Torah."

However, if two people sit together and do speak words of Torah, then *Hashem's* Presence rests between them — as the *Navi* (*Malachi* 3:16) writes, "When those who fear *Hashem* spoke to one another, *Hashem* listened and heard, and had their words written in a book of remembrance about those who fear *Hashem* and think about Him."

מֵאַיִן בָּאתָ? — מִטִּפָּה סְרוּחָה.
וּלְאָן אַתָּה הוֹלֵךְ? — לִמְקוֹם עָפָר, רִמָּה וְתוֹלֵעָה.
וְלִפְנֵי מִי אַתָּה עָתִיד לִתֵּן דִּין וְחֶשְׁבּוֹן? — לִפְנֵי מֶלֶךְ מַלְכֵי הַמְּלָכִים, הַקָּדוֹשׁ בָּרוּךְ הוּא.

[ב] רַבִּי חֲנִינָא סְגַן הַכֹּהֲנִים אוֹמֵר: הֱוֵי מִתְפַּלֵּל בִּשְׁלוֹמָהּ שֶׁל מַלְכוּת, שֶׁאִלְמָלֵא מוֹרָאָהּ, אִישׁ אֶת רֵעֵהוּ חַיִּים בְּלָעוֹ.

[ג] רַבִּי חֲנִינָא בֶּן תְּרַדְיוֹן אוֹמֵר: שְׁנַיִם שֶׁיּוֹשְׁבִין וְאֵין בֵּינֵיהֶם דִּבְרֵי תוֹרָה, הֲרֵי זֶה מוֹשַׁב לֵצִים, שֶׁנֶּאֱמַר: "וּבְמוֹשַׁב לֵצִים לֹא יָשָׁב . . .".
אֲבָל שְׁנַיִם שֶׁיּוֹשְׁבִין וְיֵשׁ בֵּינֵיהֶם דִּבְרֵי תוֹרָה, שְׁכִינָה שְׁרוּיָה בֵינֵיהֶם — שֶׁנֶּאֱמַר, "אָז נִדְבְּרוּ יִרְאֵי ה' אִישׁ אֶל רֵעֵהוּ, וַיַּקְשֵׁב ה' וַיִּשְׁמָע, וַיִּכָּתֵב סֵפֶר זִכָּרוֹן לְפָנָיו, לְיִרְאֵי ה' וּלְחֹשְׁבֵי שְׁמוֹ."

מִטִּפָּה סְרוּחָה — From a tiny cell that could have easily spoiled.

Before a baby is born, it begins as a tiny cell, as small as the point of a pin. For nine months that cell grows and grows until it become a full-sized baby. But if *Hashem* didn't allow this tiny cell to begin growing, it would have spoiled and melted away.

A person should always remember that he was once just a tiny cell that could have easily spoiled. If he thinks this way, he will never be guilty of too much pride.

לִמְקוֹם עָפָר רִמָּה וְתוֹלֵעָה — To a place of dust, where even tiny worms are stronger than the strongest man.

A person does not live forever. He is like a traveler going from place to place. A traveler does not bring his furniture and all of his finery with him when he travels. A suitcase or two is all he takes with him. He must learn to be satisfied with a little.

When a person goes on to his new life, his fancy house and car do not go with him. He must leave behind all of his beautiful clothing and elegant furniture. His servants and maids do not accompany him. The only luggage he can take along is his *mitzvos* and good deeds.

A person who thinks this way will be saved from תַּאֲוָה,

and from all the sinfulness that it can lead to.

לִפְנֵי מֶלֶךְ מַלְכֵי הַמְּלָכִים — Before Hashem, the King of kings.

Finally, a person who always remembers that he will stand in judgment before *Hashem* will carefully consider everything he does. This will prevent him from sinning. And, even more, it will cause him to seek *mitzvos*. This is why David *Hamelech* (King David) taught us, "שִׁוִּיתִי ה' לְנֶגְדִּי תָמִיד, I always have placed *Hashem* in front of me" (*Tehillim* 16:8).

2. אִישׁ אֶת רֵעֵהוּ חַיִּים בְּלָעוֹ — They would swallow each other alive.

The government keeps things in order and peaceful. People, who otherwise might commit crime, don't, because they are afraid that the government's police force will catch them and punish them.

The *Gemara* (*Avodah Zarah* 4b) teaches that without government people would act like fish. In the sea there are no policemen. Any fish can do whatever he wants to. And so, larger fish swallow up smaller fish. Then the larger fish are swallowed up by even larger ones. If there were no government to control people, they would act the same way. The stronger person would take everything away from the weaker person, until an even stronger person would come along and take everything away from him.

. . . written in a book of remembrance . . .

Now you may ask, "This lesson only teaches us about two people who discuss the Torah. How do we know that *Hashem* gives a reward even to one person who sits by himself and studies Torah?"

The answer to this question is found in *Megillas Eichah* (3:28), "Although he sits alone and studies in silence, he will receive a reward for what he does."

4. R' Shimon taught:

If three people ate at one table and they did not speak any words of Torah, it is as if they ate the sacrifices of dead idols — as the *Navi* (*Yeshayahu* 28:8) writes: "For all the tables are full of vomit and filth, when *Hashem* is not mentioned."

אֵין לִי אֶלָּא שְׁנַיִם; מִנַּיִן שֶׁאֲפִלּוּ אֶחָד שֶׁיּוֹשֵׁב וְעוֹסֵק בַּתּוֹרָה, שֶׁהַקָּדוֹשׁ בָּרוּךְ הוּא קוֹבֵעַ לוֹ שָׂכָר?

שֶׁנֶּאֱמַר: "יֵשֵׁב בָּדָד וְיִדֹּם, כִּי נָטַל עָלָיו."

[ד] רַבִּי שִׁמְעוֹן אוֹמֵר: שְׁלשָׁה שֶׁאָכְלוּ עַל שֻׁלְחָן אֶחָד וְלֹא אָמְרוּ עָלָיו דִּבְרֵי תוֹרָה, כְּאִלּוּ אָכְלוּ מִזִּבְחֵי מֵתִים, שֶׁנֶּאֱמַר: "כִּי כָּל שֻׁלְחָנוֹת מָלְאוּ קִיא צוֹאָה, בְּלִי מָקוֹם."

---

4. קִיא צוֹאָה — **Vomit and filth.**
This is how the *Navi* describes idols.

מָקוֹם — **Hashem.**
God is often called הַמָּקוֹם which means "The Place." This is because God is in every possible place. There is no place in the world without Him. In fact, He is even bigger than the world. This is why the *Midrash* calls *Hashem* the Place of the world.

. . . and they did speak words of Torah . . .

However, if three people ate at one table and they did speak words of Torah there, it is as if they ate from *Hashem's* table — as the *Navi (Yechezkel* 4:22) writes: "And he spoke of Me; this is the table that is before *Hashem.*"

אֲבָל שְׁלֹשָׁה שֶׁאָכְלוּ עַל שֻׁלְחָן אֶחָד וְאָמְרוּ עָלָיו דִּבְרֵי תוֹרָה, כְּאִלּוּ אָכְלוּ מִשֻּׁלְחָנוֹ שֶׁל מָקוֹם, שֶׁנֶּאֱמַר: ,,וַיְדַבֵּר אֵלַי, זֶה הַשֻּׁלְחָן אֲשֶׁר לִפְנֵי ה׳.''

5. R' Chanina ben Chachinai taught:

If a person is awake at night or travels alone on the road, and turns his heart to worthless thoughts, then he can blame only himself if anything bad happens to him.

6. R' Nechunia ben Hakanah taught:

Any person who accepts the yoke of Torah, will be excused from the yoke of the government and from the yoke of a job.

However, any person who removes the yoke of Torah from himself will have the yoke of the government and the yoke of a job placed upon him.

7. R' Chalafta ben Dosa of Kfar Chanania taught:

If ten people sit together studying the Torah, then *Hashem's* Presence rests among them — as it is written in *Tehillim* (82:1), "God stands in the *minyan* of *tzaddikim* who are strong in the Torah's ways."

How do we know that *Hashem* joins even five people who study Torah together? The *Navi* (*Amos* 9:6) writes, "He, God, has set up His bundle upon earth."

How do we know that *Hashem* joins even three people who study Torah together? It is written in *Tehillim* (82:1), "He, God, judges together with the judges of the *beis din.*"

[ה] רַבִּי חֲנִינָא בֶּן חֲכִינַאי אוֹמֵר: הַנֵּעוֹר בַּלַּיְלָה, וְהַמְהַלֵּךְ בַּדֶּרֶךְ יְחִידִי, וּמְפַנֶּה לִבּוֹ לְבַטָּלָה — הֲרֵי זֶה מִתְחַיֵּב בְּנַפְשׁוֹ.

[ו] רַבִּי נְחוּנְיָא בֶּן הַקָּנָה אוֹמֵר: כָּל הַמְקַבֵּל עָלָיו עֹל תּוֹרָה, מַעֲבִירִין מִמֶּנּוּ עֹל מַלְכוּת וְעֹל דֶּרֶךְ אֶרֶץ; וְכָל הַפּוֹרֵק מִמֶּנּוּ עֹל תּוֹרָה, נוֹתְנִין עָלָיו עֹל מַלְכוּת וְעֹל דֶּרֶךְ אֶרֶץ.

[ז] רַבִּי חֲלַפְתָּא בֶּן דּוֹסָא אִישׁ כְּפַר חֲנַנְיָא אוֹמֵר: עֲשָׂרָה שֶׁיּוֹשְׁבִין וְעוֹסְקִין בַּתּוֹרָה, שְׁכִינָה שְׁרוּיָה בֵינֵיהֶם, שֶׁנֶּאֱמַר, "אֱלֹהִים נִצָּב בַּעֲדַת אֵל." וּמִנַּיִן אֲפִילוּ חֲמִשָּׁה? שֶׁנֶּאֱמַר, "וַאֲגֻדָּתוֹ עַל אֶרֶץ יְסָדָהּ." וּמִנַּיִן אֲפִילוּ שְׁלֹשָׁה? שֶׁנֶּאֱמַר, "בְּקֶרֶב אֱלֹהִים יִשְׁפֹּט."

5. הֲרֵי זֶה מִתְחַיֵּב בְּנַפְשׁוֹ — **He can blame only himself if anything bad happens to him.**

Torah study and thoughts about Torah protect a person from two types of harm. First, when someone speaks and thinks words of Torah, he creates *malachim* (angels) that watch over him. Second, a mind filled with Torah does not have room for sinful thoughts.

Night time is usually peaceful and quiet. It is a wonderful time to concentrate on Torah study without being interrupted. Someone who wastes such precious time by filling his mind with nonsense, may soon find his head full of sinful thoughts.

All roads present some sort of danger — drunk drivers, broken pavement, wild animals. That is why *Hashem* sends His *malachim* to accompany a traveler, as it is written in *Tehillim* (91:11), "*Hashem* will command His angels for you, to protect you in all your ways." These *malachim* are created by the Torah that a person studies. If a person travels alone, he places himself in danger. If he thinks Torah thoughts, he protects himself.

6. עֹל תּוֹרָה . . . עֹל מַלְכוּת וְעֹל דֶּרֶךְ אֶרֶץ — **The yoke of Torah . . . the yoke of the government and the yoke of a job.**

Accepting the "yoke of Torah" means dedicating every possible moment to the study of Torah. The "yoke of the government" refers to the oppressive and harsh demands that some governments make on their prople. The "yoke of

a job" is a person's responsibility to work at a job in order to earn enough money to support himself and his family.

One who accepts the yoke of Torah is freed from the other two burdens. As we will learn later (chapter 6, *mishnah* 2), "There is no truly free man, except one who devotes himself to the study of Torah." This means that even if the person must hold a job to support his family, he should make a super-human effort to study Torah whenever he can. In return, *Hashem* will supply his needs in a super-natural way. The more time a man dedicates to Torah study, the less effort he will have to spend on earning a living. The same is true about the "yoke of government," because *Hashem* will protect him against its harshness.

7. חֲמִשָּׁה . . . וַאֲגֻדָּתוֹ — **Five . . . His bundle.**

An אֲגֻדָּה is a bundle carried in one hand. Therefore the word אֲגֻדָּה is sometimes used to described the five fingers of one hand. *Hashem's* "bundle" means a group of five people studying Torah together.

שְׁלֹשָׁה . . . אֱלֹהִים — **Three . . . the judges of the beis din.**

The word אֱלֹהִים usually means God. But sometimes it means judges, especially the judges of a *beis din*, as a Torah court is called. And a *beis din* usually has three judges. So this verse teaches us that when the judges (three people) are deciding the Torah law (and speaking words of Torah), *Hashem* joins them.

How do we know that *Hashem* joins even two people who study Torah together? The *Navi* (*Malachi* 3:16) writes, "When those who fear *Hashem* spoke to one another, *Hashem* listened and heard."

And how do we know that *Hashem* joins even one person who studies Torah by himself? It is written in the Torah (*Shemos* 20:21), "In every place where I have My Name mentioned, I will come to you and bless you."

8. R' Elazar of Bartosa taught:

Spend money for mitzvos and you will be giving *Hashem* what belongs to Him; because you and all that you own belong to Him. This is what David *Hamelech* meant when he said (*I Divrei Hayamim* 29:14), "Everything comes from You, and whatever we have given You comes from Your hand."

9. R' Yaakov taught:

If someone travels on the road reviewing his Torah lessons, but stops his review and says, "What a beautiful tree this is!" or, "What a beautiful field this is!" the Torah teaches that he can blame only himself if bad things happen to him.

וּמִנַּיִן אֲפִילוּ שְׁנַיִם? שֶׁנֶּאֱמַר, "אָז נִדְבְּרוּ יִרְאֵי ה' אִישׁ אֶל רֵעֵהוּ וַיַּקְשֵׁב ה' וַיִּשְׁמָע".

וּמִנַּיִן אֲפִילוּ אֶחָד? שֶׁנֶּאֱמַר: "בְּכָל הַמָּקוֹם אֲשֶׁר אַזְכִּיר אֶת שְׁמִי, אָבוֹא אֵלֶיךָ וּבֵרַכְתִּיךָ".

[ח] רַבִּי אֶלְעָזָר אִישׁ בַּרְתּוֹתָא אוֹמֵר: תֶּן לוֹ מִשֶּׁלוֹ, שֶׁאַתָּה וְשֶׁלְּךָ שֶׁלּוֹ; וְכֵן בְּדָוִד הוּא אוֹמֵר: "כִּי מִמְּךָ הַכֹּל, וּמִיָּדְךָ נָתַנּוּ לָךְ".

[ט] רַבִּי יַעֲקֹב אוֹמֵר: הַמְהַלֵּךְ בַּדֶּרֶךְ וְשׁוֹנֶה, וּמַפְסִיק מִמִּשְׁנָתוֹ, וְאוֹמֵר: "מַה נָּאֶה אִילָן זֶה וּמַה נָּאֶה נִיר זֶה" — מַעֲלֶה עָלָיו הַכָּתוּב כְּאִלּוּ מִתְחַיֵּב בְּנַפְשׁוֹ.

---

8. רַבִּי אֶלְעָזָר אִישׁ בַּרְתּוֹתָא — **R' Elazar of Bartosa.**

This *Tanna* was well known as a very charitable man. The *Gemara* (*Taanis* 24a) says that he used to give much more money than he should have. In fact, whenever the town's official *tzedakah gabbaim* (charity collectors) saw him coming, they would hide. They were afraid that he would give them every cent that he had.

One day, R' Elazar was on his way to the market to buy whatever he needed for his daughter's wedding. The *gabbaim* saw him and ran to hide, but it was too late. He had spotted them first. He ran after them. When he caught up with them, he asked, "For what are you collecting?"

They said, "There is a poor orphan boy who is engaged to a poor orphan girl. They have no money for their wedding."

"How much money do you still need?" R' Elazar asked. When they told him the amount, he said, "Why I just happen to have that much with me. Here, take it. The two orphans are much more important than my daughter."

Now R' Elazar had given them almost all the money he had. Only one coin remained. With that coin he bought a small amount of wheat. When he came home, he placed the wheat in his grain crib.

His daughter saw him and said, "Father, what have you bought for my wedding?"

He answered, "Whatever you find in the grain crib." Then he went to the *beis midrash* to study.

R' Elazar's daughter walked sadly to the grain crib. "All I have for my wedding is a few pieces of wheat," she thought.

Imagine how surprised she was when she saw the grain crib overflowing with wheat. *Hashem* had made a miracle to repay R' Elazar for the kindness he has shown to the two orphans.

When she saw all the wheat, she ran to the *beis midrash* to tell her father. He said, "We will sell the wheat. But we will only take enough of the money to pay for your wedding expenses. That is the amount we would give any poor girl who came to us for help in making her wedding. Any money that is left over we will give to poor people."

From this story we can understand what R' Elazar meant by, "You and all that you own belong to Him."

9. מַה נָּאֶה אִילָן זֶה — **"What a beautiful tree this is!"**

When a person sees something beautiful, he praises *Hashem* for creating such beauty in His world. But if someone is studying Torah, he should not stop to look at the beautiful things around him. A person who travels on the road places himself in a dangerous situation. If he reviews his Torah studies while traveling, he creates *malachim* (angels) who protect him from danger — as we discussed in *mishnah* 5. But if he stops his Torah study to talk about the tree, then he loses his protection. If anything bad happens to him, he has only himself to blame.

אֲפִילוּ שְׁנַיִם . . . אֲפִילוּ אֶחָד — **Even two . . . even one.**

The *mishnah* teaches us that whenever someone studies Torah, *Hashem* comes to join in. So why does the *mishnah* first speak of ten, then five, then three, two and one? This teaches us that the more people that learn Torah together, the better.

10. R' Dostai bar Yannai taught this lesson that he learned from R' Meir:

Any person who forgets a part of his Torah learning can blame only himself if bad things happen to him. This is what the Torah means by the sentence *(Devarim* 4:9), "Just beware! Watch your soul very carefully! Do not forget those things that your eyes have seen!"

Is this true even if the lesson was too difficult for him to remember? No, it does not apply to a very difficult lesson, as the same Torah sentence continues, "And do not remove them from your heart all the days of your life." From this sentence we see that a person is only responsible if he sits by lazily and does not review his lessons. Then he is to blame for forgetting them.

11. R' Chanina ben Dosa taught:

Anyone whose fear of sin is more important to him than his wisdom, his wisdom will remain with him. But anyone whose wisdom is more important to him than his fear of sin, his wisdom will not remain with him.

12. He also taught:

Anyone whose deeds are greater than his wisdom, his wisdom will remain with him. But anyone whose wisdom is greater than his deeds, his wisdom will not remain with him.

13. He also taught:

Anyone who is pleasing to other people, is pleasing also to God. And anyone who is not pleasing to other people, is not pleasing to God.

14. R' Dosa ben Harkinas taught:

Sleeping late in the morning, drinking wine in the afternoon, chattering childishly, and sitting in gatherings of ignorant people — all of these remove a person from the world.

[י] רַבִּי דוֹסְתָּאי בַּר יַנַּאי מִשׁוּם רַבִּי מֵאִיר אוֹמֵר: כָּל הַשּׁוֹכֵחַ דָּבָר אֶחָד מִמִּשְׁנָתוֹ, מַעֲלֶה עָלָיו הַכָּתוּב כְּאִלּוּ מִתְחַיֵּב בְּנַפְשׁוֹ. שֶׁנֶּאֱמַר, "רַק הִשָּׁמֶר לְךָ, וּשְׁמֹר נַפְשְׁךָ מְאֹד, פֶּן תִּשְׁכַּח אֶת הַדְּבָרִים אֲשֶׁר רָאוּ עֵינֶיךָ." יָכוֹל אֲפִילוּ תָקְפָה עָלָיו מִשְׁנָתוֹ? תַּלְמוּד לוֹמַר, "וּפֶן יָסוּרוּ מִלְּבָבְךָ כֹּל יְמֵי חַיֶּיךָ." הָא אֵינוֹ מִתְחַיֵּב בְּנַפְשׁוֹ עַד שֶׁיֵּשֵׁב וִיסִירֵם מִלִּבּוֹ.

[יא] רַבִּי חֲנִינָא בֶּן דּוֹסָא אוֹמֵר: כָּל שֶׁיִּרְאַת חֶטְאוֹ קוֹדֶמֶת לְחָכְמָתוֹ, חָכְמָתוֹ מִתְקַיֶּמֶת. וְכָל שֶׁחָכְמָתוֹ קוֹדֶמֶת לְיִרְאַת חֶטְאוֹ, אֵין חָכְמָתוֹ מִתְקַיֶּמֶת.

[יב] הוּא הָיָה אוֹמֵר: כָּל שֶׁמַּעֲשָׂיו מְרֻבִּין מֵחָכְמָתוֹ, חָכְמָתוֹ מִתְקַיֶּמֶת. וְכָל שֶׁחָכְמָתוֹ מְרֻבָּה מִמַּעֲשָׂיו, אֵין חָכְמָתוֹ מִתְקַיֶּמֶת.

[יג] הוּא הָיָה אוֹמֵר: כָּל שֶׁרוּחַ הַבְּרִיּוֹת נוֹחָה הֵימֶנּוּ, רוּחַ הַמָּקוֹם נוֹחָה הֵימֶנּוּ. וְכָל שֶׁאֵין רוּחַ הַבְּרִיּוֹת נוֹחָה הֵימֶנּוּ, אֵין רוּחַ הַמָּקוֹם נוֹחָה הֵימֶנּוּ.

[יד] רַבִּי דוֹסָא בֶּן הָרְכִּינַס אוֹמֵר: שֵׁנָה שֶׁל שַׁחֲרִית, וְיַיִן שֶׁל צָהֳרַיִם, וְשִׂיחַת הַיְלָדִים, וִישִׁיבַת בָּתֵּי כְנֵסִיּוֹת שֶׁל עַמֵּי הָאָרֶץ — מוֹצִיאִין אֶת הָאָדָם מִן הָעוֹלָם.

11-12. ... כָּל שֶׁיִּרְאַת חֶטְאוֹ ... כָּל שֶׁמַּעֲשָׂיו — **Anyone whose fear of sin . . . Anyone whose deeds.**

A person should study Torah in order to know how to perform *mitzvos* and how to keep away from sin. If someone does this, his Torah knowledge will remain with him, because he will always practice what he studies.

But if someone doesn't practice the Torah laws that he studies, he will soon stop studying. And he will lose whatever Torah wisdom he has gained.

Mishnah 11 and *mishnah* 12 teach almost the same lesson; except that *mishnah* 11 speaks about not sinning, while *mishnah* 12 speaks about doing *mitzvos*.

14. שֵׁנָה שֶׁל שַׁחֲרִית — **Sleeping late in the morning.**

Earlier (chapter 2, *Mishnah* 18) we learned that we must always be careful to recite the *Shema* and *Shemoneh Esrei* at their proper times. Our *mishnah* now tells us how bad it is to oversleep these times.

מוֹצִיאִין אֶת הָאָדָם מִן הָעוֹלָם — **Remove a person from the world.**

The activities listed in this *Mishnah* are all ways of wasting precious time. They stop us from doing the things we were created to do.

15. R' Elazar Hamodai taught:

Someone who treats holy things without respect, or who treats *Yomim Tovim* (Festivals) as weekdays, or who shames another person in public, or who denies the holiness of the *mitzvah* of *bris milah* (circumcision) that *Hashem* taught to Avraham *Avinu*, or who explains the Torah in a way that is against *halachah* — even if he has Torah knowledge and good deeds, that person has no share in the World to Come.

16. R' Yishmael taught:

You should be ready to serve an elderly wise man, be nice to a younger person, and greet everybody with joy.

17. R' Akiva taught:

Joking and making fun lead a person to sinfulness.

The Unwritten Torah is a fence that protects the Written Torah.

Separating *maaser* from your crop is a fence that protects your wealth.

Promises are a fence that protects you from the desire for unnecessary things.

The fence that protects wisdom is silence.

[טו] רַבִּי אֶלְעָזָר הַמּוֹדָעִי אוֹמֵר: הַמְחַלֵּל אֶת הַקֳּדָשִׁים, וְהַמְבַזֶּה אֶת הַמּוֹעֲדוֹת, וְהַמַּלְבִּין פְּנֵי חֲבֵרוֹ בָּרַבִּים, וְהַמֵּפֵר בְּרִיתוֹ שֶׁל אַבְרָהָם אָבִינוּ, וְהַמְגַלֶּה פָנִים בַּתּוֹרָה שֶׁלֹּא כַהֲלָכָה, אַף עַל פִּי שֶׁיֵּשׁ בְּיָדוֹ תּוֹרָה וּמַעֲשִׂים טוֹבִים — אֵין לוֹ חֵלֶק לָעוֹלָם הַבָּא.

[טז] רַבִּי יִשְׁמָעֵאל אוֹמֵר: הֱוֵי קַל לְרֹאשׁ, וְנוֹחַ לְתִשְׁחֹרֶת, וֶהֱוֵי מְקַבֵּל אֶת כָּל הָאָדָם בְּשִׂמְחָה.

[יז] רַבִּי עֲקִיבָא אוֹמֵר: שְׂחוֹק וְקַלּוּת רֹאשׁ מַרְגִּילִין אֶת הָאָדָם לְעֶרְוָה. מָסוֹרֶת סְיָג לַתּוֹרָה. מַעַשְׂרוֹת סְיָג לָעֹשֶׁר. נְדָרִים סְיָג לַפְּרִישׁוּת. סְיָג לַחָכְמָה שְׁתִיקָה.

---

15. . . . הַמְחַלֵּל אֶת הַקֳּדָשִׁים — **Someone who treats holy things without respect . . .**

Hashem created the world and placed many kinds of holiness into it. There is **the holiness of place** — for example, the *Beis Hamikdash* and the *korbanos* (sacrifices) offered there — the *mishnah* calls these קֳדָשִׁים, holy things; **the holiness of time** — such as *Yomim Tovim*; **the holiness of human beings** — the *neshamah* (soul); **the holiness of the Jewish People** — the *bris milah*; and the most holy thing in the whole world — **the holiness of the Torah.**

Anyone who treats holy places, holy days, the Torah, or even other people improperly, shows that he has no respect for *Hashem* and the things that *Hashem* considers special. Such a person does not deserve a share in *Olam Haba* (the World to Come), even if he has studied Torah and done good deeds during his lifetime.

17. שְׂחוֹק וְקַלּוּת רֹאשׁ — **Joking and making fun.**

The *mishnah* speaks of a person who is never serious. He spends his entire day laughing and fooling around. Since he thinks of life as a big joke, he will soon lose respect even for himself. Because of this he will lead himself to sinful ways.

מָסוֹרֶת — **The Unwritten Torah.**

When *Hashem* taught Moshe *Rabbeinu* (our teacher Moses) the Torah at Mount Sinai, He taught him the words as they are written in the *Sefer Torah* (Torah Scroll). But He also explained the meaning of these words to Moshe. The words of the Torah are called תּוֹרָה שֶׁבִּכְתָב, the Written Torah. The explanations are called תּוֹרָה שֶׁבְּעַל פֶּה, the

Unwritten (or Oral) Torah. Without the Unwritten Torah we would never be able to understand the Written Torah.

For many hundreds of years the Unwritten Torah was taught from memory. Each father taught his sons and each teacher taught his students by heart. Many hours were spent each day memorizing the explanations of the Written Torah. This method of passing the teachings of the Unwritten Torah from one generation to the next is called מָסוֹרֶת, *masores*, which means "handing down" or "tradition". This way of learning Torah could only continue as long as the Jewish people were living in freedom in *Eretz Yisrael*.

But during the time of the Second *Beis Hamikdash*, enemy armies conquered the land. These armies demanded heavy taxes. The people had to work long hours in order to pay these taxes. Soon they had very little time left for Torah study. And they began forgetting what they had learned.

About one hundred years after the Second *Beis Hamikdash* was destroyed, R' Yehudah Hanassi saw that all of the Unwritten Torah would soon be forgotten. He gathered together many of the remaining Torah scholars and, with their help, collected the explanations and lessons of the Unwritten Torah that they had been taught by their teachers. They wrote down these lessons and called them *Mishnah*, which means "teaching."

As time went on, more and more of the Unwritten Torah was written down. This second collection of teachings is called the *Gemara* or the *Talmud*. Other parts were written down and called *Midrash*.

The only way we can be sure that we understand the

Maaser is a fence that protects your wealth.

Written Torah is by carefully studying the *Mishnah, Gemara* and *Midrash*. Or, in other words, the תּוֹרָה שֶׁבְּעַל פֶּה is a fence that protects the תּוֹרָה שֶׁבִּכְתָב.

It is interesting to note that the *gematria*, or letter value, of the words בְּעַל פֶּה is 187 (2 + 70 + 30 + 80 + 5), and the *gematria* of בִּכְתָב is 424 (2 + 20 + 400 + 2). Together (187 + 424) these equal 611, the same *gematria* as תּוֹרָה (400 + 6 + 200 + 5).

מַעְשְׂרוֹת סְיָג לְעֹשֶׁר — **Separating maaser from your crop is a fence to protect your wealth.**

The Torah teaches that the road to riches is open to the person who gives *maaser* (see chapter 1, *mishnah* 16). By giving *maaser*, a person proves that he knows from where his crop came. He shows that all wealth really comes from God, the true Owner of everything in the world. This man deserves to be rich, because he uses his riches to serve God.

18. He also taught:

God loves man, that is why He created him in His own image. God showed Man even greater love by telling Man that God created him in His own image, as the Torah (*Bereishis* 9:6) says, "In the image of God, He made Man."

God loves the Jewish People, that is why they are called "God's children." God showed them even more love by telling them that they are called God's children, as it is written in the Torah (*Devarim* 14:1), "You are the children of *Hashem*, your God."

God loves the Jewish People, that is why He gave them a valuable present, the Torah. God showed them even more love by telling them that He gave them a valuable present, as it is written (*Mishlei* 4:2), "I have given you a good present, do not go away from My Torah."

19. Everything that a person does is seen, yet everyone is permitted to do what he wants to do.

The world is judged in a good way, everything according to how many good deeds a person has done.

20. He also taught that *Hashem* runs the world like a business:

Everything is given on trust, but this can be like a net spread to trap a person. The shop is open; the Storekeeper gives credit; the record book is open; the hand writes; and whoever wants to borrow may come and borrow. But one must remember that the collectors always make their collection rounds, whether the borrower knows about them or not; and they have good proof of what is owed. The judgment is truthful. And everything is prepared for the banquet.

[יח] הוּא הָיָה אוֹמֵר: חָבִיב אָדָם שֶׁנִּבְרָא בְּצֶלֶם. חִבָּה יְתֵרָה נוֹדַעַת לוֹ שֶׁנִּבְרָא בְּצֶלֶם, שֶׁנֶּאֱמַר, "כִּי בְּצֶלֶם אֱלֹהִים עָשָׂה אֶת הָאָדָם."
חֲבִיבִין יִשְׂרָאֵל, שֶׁנִּקְרְאוּ בָנִים לַמָּקוֹם. חִבָּה יְתֵרָה נוֹדַעַת לָהֶם שֶׁנִּקְרְאוּ בָנִים לַמָּקוֹם, שֶׁנֶּאֱמַר, "בָּנִים אַתֶּם לַה' אֱלֹהֵיכֶם."
חֲבִיבִין יִשְׂרָאֵל, שֶׁנִּתַּן לָהֶם כְּלִי חֶמְדָּה. חִבָּה יְתֵרָה נוֹדַעַת לָהֶם, שֶׁנִּתַּן לָהֶם כְּלִי חֶמְדָּה, שֶׁנֶּאֱמַר, "כִּי לֶקַח טוֹב נָתַתִּי לָכֶם, תּוֹרָתִי אַל תַּעֲזֹבוּ."

[יט] הַכֹּל צָפוּי, וְהָרְשׁוּת נְתוּנָה. וּבְטוֹב הָעוֹלָם נָדוֹן, וְהַכֹּל לְפִי רֹב הַמַּעֲשֶׂה.

[כ] הוּא הָיָה אוֹמֵר: הַכֹּל נָתוּן בָּעֵרָבוֹן, וּמְצוּדָה פְרוּסָה עַל כָּל הַחַיִּים. הַחֲנוּת פְּתוּחָה; וְהַחֶנְוָנִי מַקִּיף; וְהַפִּנְקָס פָּתוּחַ; וְהַיָּד כּוֹתֶבֶת; וְכָל הָרוֹצֶה לִלְווֹת יָבֹא וְיִלְוֶה. וְהַגַּבָּאִים מַחֲזִירִין תָּדִיר בְּכָל יוֹם וְנִפְרָעִין מִן הָאָדָם, מִדַּעְתּוֹ וְשֶׁלֹּא מִדַּעְתּוֹ; וְיֵשׁ לָהֶם עַל מַה שֶׁיִּסְמְכוּ. וְהַדִּין דִּין אֱמֶת. וְהַכֹּל מְתֻקָּן לִסְעוּדָה.

---

18. חִבָּה יְתֵרָה — **Even greater love.**

When you do a favor for another person, you show that you love that person. But if the other person does not know about the favor, he will not be able to share your love.

When you do a favor for another person and you let him know what you have done, you show even more love for that person, because now he will be able to share your love.

19. הַכֹּל צָפוּי וְהָרְשׁוּת נְתוּנָה — **Everything that a person does is seen, yet everyone is permitted to do what he wants to do.**

We have learned at the beginning of chapter 2, that "An Eye sees and an Ear hears" everything that we do or say. Yet this does not force us to do the right thing. Everyone is free to do whatever he wants, whether it is right or wrong, good or bad. But you also must remember (as we have learned at the beginning of this chapter) "before Whom you will have to explain all of your actions." And you will be judged according to those actions.

20. הַכֹּל נָתוּן בָּעֵרָבוֹן — **Everything is given on trust . . .**

Whatever a person owns has been lent to him by *Hashem*. If he forgets the true Owner, then he will fall into "the trap" that will lead to pain and even death.

The "store," that is, the world, is open and full of many different items. The "Storekeeper," *Hashem*, lets everyone take what he wants. But the record book is open and each person's deeds are being written down. And "the collectors" always go around to punish those who do not fulfill their part of the trust. Yet, in the end, even those who were punished will join in "the banquet" of the World to Come, in reward for their good deeds.

21. R' Elazar ben Azaryah taught:

Without Torah, a person cannot do his job honestly; without a job, he cannot learn Torah.

Without wisdom, a person cannot fear God; without fear of God, he cannot become wise.

Without knowledge, a person cannot understand things on his own; without understanding, he cannot gain knowledge.

Without food, a person cannot learn Torah; without Torah, what purpose does his food have?

22. He also taught:

Anyone whose wisdom is greater than his deeds — what is he like? He is like a tree with many branches and few roots. When the wind blows, it will uproot the tree and turn it upside-down. This is what the *Navi* (*Yirmiyahu* 17:6) said, "He will be like a single tree in a dry land; he will not notice when good times come along. He will live on parched soil in the desert, a salty land where no people live."

But anyone whose deeds are greater than his wisdom — what is he like? He is like a tree with few branches and many roots. Even when all the winds in the world blow against it, they will not move it from its place. This is what the *Navi* (*Yirmiyahu* 17:8) said, "He will be like a tree planted near the water, with its roots spreading toward the stream. It will not notice when hot weather comes along, its leaves will remain fresh. In a rainless year it will not worry; and it will not stop giving fruit."

23. R' Elazar ben Chisma taught:

The rules about bird offerings and about husband and wife relationships are among the most important Torah laws. But astronomy and mathematics are only introductions to wisdom.

[כא] רַבִּי אֶלְעָזָר בֶּן עֲזַרְיָה אוֹמֵר: אִם אֵין תּוֹרָה, אֵין דֶּרֶךְ אֶרֶץ; אִם אֵין דֶּרֶךְ אֶרֶץ, אֵין תּוֹרָה. אִם אֵין חָכְמָה, אֵין יִרְאָה; אִם אֵין יִרְאָה, אֵין חָכְמָה. אִם אֵין דַּעַת, אֵין בִּינָה; אִם אֵין בִּינָה, אֵין דַּעַת. אִם אֵין קֶמַח, אֵין תּוֹרָה; אִם אֵין תּוֹרָה, אֵין קֶמַח.

[כב] הוּא הָיָה אוֹמֵר: כֹּל שֶׁחָכְמָתוֹ מְרֻבָּה מִמַּעֲשָׂיו — לְמָה הוּא דוֹמֶה? לְאִילָן שֶׁעֲנָפָיו מְרֻבִּין וְשָׁרָשָׁיו מוּעָטִין. וְהָרוּחַ בָּאָה, וְעוֹקַרְתּוּ וְהוֹפַכְתּוּ עַל פָּנָיו. שֶׁנֶּאֱמַר, "וְהָיָה כְּעַרְעָר בָּעֲרָבָה; וְלֹא יִרְאֶה כִּי יָבוֹא טוֹב. וְשָׁכַן חֲרֵרִים בַּמִּדְבָּר, אֶרֶץ מְלֵחָה וְלֹא תֵשֵׁב."

אֲבָל כֹּל שֶׁמַּעֲשָׂיו מְרֻבִּין מֵחָכְמָתוֹ — לְמָה הוּא דוֹמֶה? לְאִילָן שֶׁעֲנָפָיו מוּעָטִין וְשָׁרָשָׁיו מְרֻבִּין. שֶׁאֲפִילוּ כָּל הָרוּחוֹת שֶׁבָּעוֹלָם בָּאוֹת וְנוֹשְׁבוֹת בּוֹ, אֵין מְזִיזִין אוֹתוֹ מִמְּקוֹמוֹ. שֶׁנֶּאֱמַר: "וְהָיָה כְּעֵץ שָׁתוּל עַל מַיִם, וְעַל יוּבַל יְשַׁלַּח שָׁרָשָׁיו. וְלֹא יִרְאֶה כִּי יָבֹא חֹם, וְהָיָה עָלֵהוּ רַעֲנָן. וּבִשְׁנַת בַּצֹּרֶת לֹא יִדְאָג; וְלֹא יָמִישׁ מֵעֲשׂוֹת פֶּרִי."

[כג] רַבִּי אֶלְעָזָר בֶּן חִסְמָא אוֹמֵר: קִנִּין וּפִתְחֵי נִדָּה הֵן הֵן גּוּפֵי הֲלָכוֹת. תְּקוּפוֹת וְגִמַּטְרִיָּאוֹת פַּרְפְּרָאוֹת לַחָכְמָה.

---

21. תּוֹרָה . . . דֶּרֶךְ אֶרֶץ — **Torah . . . job.**
This was discussed in chapter 2, *mishnah* 2.

בִּינָה . . . דַּעַת — **Knowledge . . . understanding.**
Having דַּעַת, knowledge, means knowing how and why something works or happens. Having בִּינָה, understanding, means being able to understand one thing from another.

23. רַבִּי אֶלְעָזָר בֶּן חִסְמָא — **R' Elazar ben Chisma.**
This *Tanna* was one of the world's greatest mathematicians. Yet he taught that the main importance of astronomy

and mathematics is using them as an aid to studying Torah law. The laws about קִנִּין, and נִדָּה are often very complicated and require a good knowledge of arithmetic. Ignorant people may think that these matters are not important Torah laws, but just examples for math experts. Or, if these foolish people see the rabbis working out the numbers, they may think that mathematics is more important than Torah study. To prevent these mistakes, R' Elazar tells us which study is only an introduction, and which is truly important.

Glossary

Aharon — Aaron, the first *Kohein,* brother of Moshe *Rabbeinu*

Avinu — "Our father," title given to Avraham, Yitzchak and Yaakov, the three Patriarchs

Avodah Zarah — a volume of the Talmud

Avraham — Abraham

beis din — court of Torah law

Beis Hamikdash — the Holy Temple that stood in Yerushalayim

beis midrash — study hall

Berachos — a volume of the Talmud

Bereishis — The Book of Genesis

Chaggai — the propet Haggai

chillul Hashem — desecration of God's Holy Name

David Hamelech — King David

Devarim — the Book of Deuteronomy

Devorah — the Prophet Deborah

Divrei Hayamim — the Book of Chronicles

Eichah — the Book of Lamentations

Eliyahu — the Prophet Elijah

Eretz Yisrael — the Land of Israel

Gan Eden — Garden of Eden; Paradise

Gehinnom — Hell

Gemara — the part of the Talmud that explains and elaborates on the *Mishnah*

halachah — (a) the body of Jewish law; (b) an individual law

Hanassi — "the Prince;" title given to Rabbi Yehudah, compiler of the *Mishnah*

Hashem — God

Hatzaddik — "the righteous;" a title given to certain exceptionally righteous people

Kesubos — a volume of the Talmud

Kohein — male descendant of the priestly family of Aharon

Kohein Gadol — chief *Kohein* in the *Beis Hamikdash*

Koheles — the Book of Ecclesiastes

lashon hara — evil talk, gossip, slander, etc.

Levi — Levite

ma'aser — tithe

Makkos — a volume of the Talmud

malachim — angels

Megillah — (a) the book of Esther; (b) a volume of the Talmud

Megillas Eichah — the Book of Lamentations

middah (middos) — character trait(s)

Midrash — collections of the Sages' teachings not included in the Talmud

minyan — ten adult Jewish men, the number needed for public prayer

Mishlei — the Book of Proverbs

mishnah (mishnayos) — (a) [capitalized] the collected teachings of the Tannaim; (b) a paragraph of the *Mishnah*

mitzvah (mitzvos) — (a) Torah commandment or Torah law; (b) in general, any good deed

Moshe — Moses

Navi — Prophet

Neviim — Prophets

Olam Haba — the World to Come

Pesachim — a volume of the Talmud

Rabbeinu — "Our teacher," a title given to Moshe

rav — rabbi

Rus — Ruth

Sanhedrin — the Great Court of seventy-one judges which was the highest Torah authority until about two centuries after the destruction of the second *Beis Hamikdash*

Shabbos — the Sabbath

Shacharis — morning prayers

Shechinah — God's Holy Presence

Shema — the declaration (*Devarim* 6:4) of God's Oneness and Mastery recited along with other prayers and verses every morning and evening

Shemoneh Esrei — the Eighteen Blessings or *Amidah* that form the core of all regular prayer services

Shemos — the Book of Exodus

Shimshon — Samson

Shlomo Hamelech — King Solomon

Shmuel — the Prophet Samuel

Sotah — a volume of the Talmud

Ta'anis — a volume of the Talmud

Talmud — the teachings of the Sages who lived during and after the second *Beis Hamikdash* (until about four hundred fifty years after the destruction), containing the *Mishnah* and the *Gemara*

Tanna (-im) — Sage(s) of the *Mishnah*

Tehillim — the Book of Psalms

teshuvah — repentance

tzaddik (-im) — righteous person

tzedakah — charity

Yaakov — Jacob

Yechezkel — the Prophet Ezekiel

Yehoshua — (a) Joshua, disciple of Moses; (b) the Book of Joshua

Yerushalayim — Jerusalem

Yerushalmi — a section of the Talmud

yetzer hara — inclination towards evil

Yirmiyahu — the prophet Jeremiah

Yishayahu — the Prophet Isaiah

Yitzchak — Isaac

Yoel — the Prophet Joel

Yom (-im) Tov (-im) — Festival(s)

Yonah — the Prophet Jonah